WHO IS THE BIGGEST BULLY OF ALL?

BOOK 1 : LOCKOUTS & MANDATES
"Why Are We Harming Our Children?"

BOOK 2: CONTENT & CHARACTER
"What Are We Teaching Our Children?"

BOOK 3 :CULTURE WAR
"Why Are We Confusing Our Children?"

WHO IS THE BIGGEST BULLY OF ALL?

Especially for Parents & Grandparents

Copyright ©2022 by A. J. Lactaoen.
All rights reserved.

Permission to reproduce or transmit in any form or by any means, electronic or mechanical, including photocopying and recording or by an information storage and retrieval system, must be obtained by writing to the publisher at the address below.

Midwest Distribution:
Lincolnshire Court, Carol Stream, Illinois 60188

West Coast Distribution:
SE Whalesong Drive, Depoe Bay, Oregon 97341

Additional BOOKS by A. J. Lactaoen
911-The Red Book for Emergencies; Active Shooter Threat in Our Schools; Active Shooter Threat in Our Workplace;
101 Urban Survival

TO ORDER: Available on Amazon, Leadership Books and most Book stores

ONLINE SHOPPING: 911seminars.com under Shopping Books

LEGACY BOOKS are available at special quantity discounts to use as fundraisers, premiums, gifts or for use in corporate sales promotions. For more information, call toll free 800.721.8222; email: 911@911seminars.com or write The Independents Group Press, 7040 Hawaii Kai Drive #26435, Honolulu, HI 96825.

ISBN 978-0-9771577-3-0

Publisher's Cataloging-in-Publication Data

Lactaoen, A. J.

Who is the Biggest Bully of All?: Especially for Parents & Grandparents

p.c. Includes bibliographical references and index.

ISBN 978-0-9771577-3-0

1. Education 2. Parenting 3. Self-help – United States

WHO IS THE BIGGEST BULLY OF ALL?

Pull Back the Curtain & Expose the Bullies Who Control Your Life

---

A. J. Lactaoen

ABOUT

We begin, appropriately with questions. Throughout this treatise, we pose questions that must be asked. We offer some suggestions but in the end, only you know the answer.

Who?

This work is not written for academics or so called experts. Thus, we use no footnotes or include an exhaustive list of resources. This is written especially for Parents and Grandparents who have their own street smart sense of what is on the up and up. We know that ordinary folk pay attention to the reality of what is said and not so much who says it.

What?

We discuss these 3 important topics in our 3 part series: Lockouts & Mandates; Content & Character; Culture Wars

Why?

Parents & Grandparents are the best thing between their children and harm's way. Our children are exposed to an unexpected bully – the bureaucrats who are supposed to protect them.

How?

We know that people prefer to get their "AHA" moment of understanding from looking at one picture vs. reading 50 pages, we also understand that a quotable quote is most memorable. So we use both. Enjoy.

DEDICATION

For all the children who had to endure the cruelty of lockdowns, isolation and unreasonable mandates for too long. We, the adults, failed our own children and grandchildren by not speaking up, by not making our voices heard, by not intervening sooner, by not standing up to the Bullies.

It is our responsibility now to be good examples on how to Stand Up!

Warning - Disclaimer

This book is designed to provide information and recommendations on how to improve school safety. It is sold with the understanding that the author and publisher are not engaged in offering legal, medical, accounting or other professional services of a licensed, certified professional should be acquired.

It is not the purpose of this guidebook to provide all the information necessary for school emergencies, but instead to simplify, and complement other available data.

Every effort has been made to make this guidebook as accurate and complete as possible. However, there is always the possibility of inadvertent mistakes, both typographical and in content.

Furthermore, this manual contains information that is current only up to the printing date. Please refer to future editions for updated material. The primary purpose of this book is to educate. The authors and Legacy Books (TIG) shall have neither liability nor responsibility to any person or entity with respect to any loss or damage caused, directly or indirectly, by the information contained in this book.

CONTENTS

ABOUT 4

AUTHOR'S NOTE 8

HOW TO USE THIS BOOK 10

PART 1 BECAUSE WE CARE 11

PART 2 COMMUNICATION IS KEY 39

PART 3 BULLIES 69

PART 4 LOCKOUTS AND MANDATES 95

PART 5 FIX IT! 121

LIST OF QUOTES 141

LIST OF ILLUSTRATIONS 142

BOOK 2 PREVIEW 143

BOOK 3 PREVIEW 144

Author's Note

"Love is the greatest gift that one generation can leave to another."
— Richard Garnett

We all wear different hats. Depending on our backgrounds, where we live, where we went to school, where we work, who are the friends with whom we share our joys and sorrows, where we go to worship, where we go to celebrate. All these factors and more play a key role in how we see the world.

We all have different lenses. Depending on our religious, political, social, economic, professional and/or labor affiliations.

What if we were to put aside our different hats and wear only one when dealing with our grandchildren's schools?

What if we were to just put on our Grampa and Gramma hat?

What if we were to just focus on the best path for our grandchildren in their schools during these challenging times?

Do you think we could agree on a good many things?

Do you think that Grandparents can help the children of our children through the confusion?

This is the purpose of our book. We want to help confront the unnamed Bullies in our grandchildren's lives just as we confronted the back yard bullies in their parents' youth.

We have some answers, we have some suggestions, we have some ideas and we have a lot of questions. We invite you to pose the questions you may have and share the answers so we can put some of those answers into action.

Our generation knows that time is fleeting so we need to start now.

HOW TO USE THIS BOOK

"There is no exercise better for the heart than reaching down and lifting people up"
– John Holmes

Our goal after reading this book is to be able to answer two crucial questions:

1) Does your school have the right plan, staffing and resources in place to protect, nurture and educate your child or grandchild?
2) If not, how can you help?

BECAUSE WE CARE

Learn how to use the problem solving approach in dealing with complex hurdles which arise from bureaucratic groupthink. Become a part of the solution instead of adding to the confusion. Focus on the goal to help your children.

COMMUNICATION IS KEY

Clear and constant communication is the basic requirement. Do not be distracted.

BULLIES

Bullies have many faces. Look behind the masks.

FIX IT !

We must fix the mistakes we have made in the past. We must ask the difficult questions before we can find the valuable answers. The situation determines the solution.

GO TO THE SOURCE

Take advantage of the information and programs described in this section. You may be surprised to find out how much help is available.

PART 1

BECAUSE WE CARE

"The Golden Rule of school policy is to put yourself in place of the children."

– AJL

GRATITUDE

Dear Teachers,

To those who never stopped welcoming our children into your classrooms every day, thank you.

To those who had to master a whole new world of technology using Zoom so you could keep our children up to date academically without losing their opportunity to graduate on time, thank you.

To those who had to adjust to an entirely different dynamic teaching some children on campus, while keeping many studying at home engaged at the same time, thank you.

To those who understood that our children's social skills were the most affected during this pandemic, thank you.

To those who had to fight, despite your own frustrations, to help our children cope with the bureaucracy of rules, thank you.

To those who showed our children the little acts of affection through the twinkle in their eyes or a quick peek of a friendly face behind the mask, thank you.

"I awoke this morning with devout thanksgiving for my friends, the old and the new."

—RWE

In the words of Emerson, I also awoke with the realization that this project would not be complete without the insightful illustrations of our premiere artist Judy Boyle and the contributions of my assistants Ally and Janette. Gratiam habeō.

DYA DO YOU AGREE?

SHOULDN'T SCHOOLS AND PARENTS WORK TOGETHER?

CONFIRMATION: IN WRITING
- Established Policies and Procedures
- Goals and Expectations for each grade
- Curriculum and Lesson Plans

COMMUNICATION:
- Easy Access to website and school material
- Contact numbers for parents in an emergency
- Contact numbers for Administration in an emergency

COOPERATION:
- School will encourage parents to participate in school activities
- School will provide a forum for all parent concerns
- School will be open and transparent to parents regarding their child.

INTRODUCTION

"You can't go back and change the beginning but you can start where you are and change the ending."

– C. S. Lewis

IT'S A MAD, MAD, MAD, MAD WORLD

Do you feel like you are having tea with Alice in Wonderland? Or maybe on a planet in the Star Trek universe where no man has gone before? Do you feel like you took a trip on a time machine that dropped you off in an alternate time warp where everything is in a flip-flop zone?

Did you ever really think that your favorite Dr. Seuss books could be banned from the elementary schools for being harmful while explicitly graphic books are now in our libraries for our K-3 children ? Two timeless classics, Pulitzer Prize author, Harper Lee's "To Kill A Mockingbird" and Mark Twain's "The Adventures of Huckleberry Finn," are now branded "racist."

What's going on, you ask?

Many of our schools, the safe harbor where the community gathers whenever there is an emergency, are now shuttered and our children are LOCKED OUT !

SOMETHING IS TERRIBLY WRONG

Our schools are the focal point of our neighborhoods. Our schools are not just brick and mortar buildings where we send our children to learn, they also serve as shelters for the community in a hurricane or flash flood, they double as centers for Adult Education, Community Programs, Musical Productions, Athletic & Robotic Tournaments, Proms and Graduations. There is no other location that has served so many people over so many generations. We even vote in person at our neighborhood school. No matter what your age, race, sex, religion or political persuasion, we are all vested in our neighborhood schools.

CHURCH

YOU

We Are All Vested

SCHOOL

In Our Neighborhood School

BUSINESS

LOCAL HOSPITAL

"All I really need to know I learned in kindergarten."
– Robert Fulghum

- Share Everything
- Play Fair
- Don't hit people
- Put things back where you found them
- Clean up your own mess
- Don't take things that aren't yours
- Say you are sorry when you hurt somebody
- Wash your hands before you eat
- Flush
- Warm cookies and cold milk are good for you
- Live a balanced life – learn some and think some and draw and paint and sing and dance and play and work every day some.
- Take a nap every afternoon.
- When you go out into the world, watch out for traffic, hold hands and stick together.
- Wonder. Remember the little seed in the Styrofoam cup. The roots go down and the plant goes up and nobody really knows how or why, but we are all like that.
- Goldfish and hamsters and white mice and even the little seed in the Styrofoam cup – they all die. So do we.
- And then remember the Dick and Jane books and the first word you learned – the biggest word of all – LOOK.
- Everything you need to know is in there somewhere. The Golden Rule and love and basic sanitation. Ecology and politics and equality and sane living.
- And it is still true, no matter how old you are – when you go out into the world, it is best to hold hands and stick together.

SOMEBODY FLUNKED KINDERGARTEN

In simpler times, everybody took for granted the main points described in Robert Fulghum's classic regarding the "Golden Rule" and sane living. Ultimately we must come to the realization that despite the importance of knowledge, we are what we do, not what we know, think or say.

Knowledge is power. The responsibility of acquiring knowledge is applying what we have learned into positive action. In that regard, too many of us flunked Kindergarten.

Question: What's the difference between a smart man and a dumb man?

Answer: Absolutely nothing. They both think they know everything.

WHY DO PEOPLE DO STUPID THINGS?

Here are some of the reasons. Maybe you can add to the list.
- Fear: Paralysis
- Laziness: No need to check if it's safe or not.
- Carelessness: Rush, rush, rush
- Fatigue: Burn out Just hope it's not your doctor, pilot, or dentist
- Social Pressure: "What will the Cool people think ?"
- Addictions: "I can't help it."
- Ignorance: "I didn't know" Ignorance is not bliss.
- Denial: "Not Me!" If you don't think it will happen to you then you won't take any precautions.
- Blame: "Somebody told me to do it!" Benjamin Franklin once said that he who is good at making excuses is seldom good for anything else.

WHERE HAVE ALL THE WISE ONES GONE?

The wisdom of the ages seems to be stranded in books stacked up on shelves in our libraries, only released in graduate theses when required, mostly relegated to footnotes that nobody reads.

So who can help prevent us from doing stupid things in a crisis?

Socrates, Plato, Aristotle, Aquinas, Augustine, Confucius are not forgotten but sorely ignored when we need their wisdom most. Instead, we get the opinions of the "experts" who tell us what we must do and how we must live.

"We should be on our guard not to overestimate science and scientific methods when it is a question of human problems, and we should not assume that experts are the only ones who have the right to express themselves on questions affecting the organization of society."

– Albert Einstein

EXPERTS

A colleague who also conducts Active Shooter Training workshops for schools once told me he doesn't believe there are any experts. If there was such a person who knows exactly what to do to solve a problem, then there would no longer be a problem.

It shouldn't surprise us that "for every expert, there is an equal and opposite expert." (Arthur C. Clarke) Robertson Davies was even more to the point. "We all create an outward self with which to face the world, and some people come to believe that is what they truly are. So they people the world with doctors who are nothing outside of the consulting room, and judges who are nothing when they are not in court, and businessmen who wither with boredom when they have to."

WHO'S IN CHARGE ?

A truck driver got the top of his semi-truck stuck under an underpass one day when he took a risk and thought he had enough clearance.

First the executives brought in a supervisor from the highway department, the supervisor immediately called an engineer. The engineer tried to figure out an elaborate way to raise the underpass up, so the truck could be freed without damage.

A little boy, named Cooper, on his way back from fishing at the nearby pond kept trying to get the engineer's attention. "Hi Sir!! Hi MISTER!" But he was ignored as the engineer's assistant yelled at him to keep back because they were doing dangerous, important work.

The highway department supervisor evaluated the engineer's plans and thought it was too complicated and too expensive, so he came up with another idea.. He called a contractor with heavy equipment , who came out to the scene and said, "Maybe if we dig out the road under the truck with a backhoe? Then it will lower the truck and it can be driven off."

"An expert is someone who knows more and more about less and less until finally he knows everything about nothing."

Cooper was jumping up and down to get the contractor's attention.. "Hi Sir!! Hi MISTER!" The contractor just scowled at the little boy. " Don't bother us now kid. We got an emergency here."

The precocious little boy wouldn't give up trying to get the truck driver's attention. "Hi Sir! Hi, MISTER!" The truck driver, who felt sorry for ignoring the kid, smiled at him and said, "What is it?"

"Mister, I know what to do!" Cooper said. "JUST LET THE AIR OUT OF THE TIRES!"

I always loved that story because it demonstrates clearly to the ones in charge, the "EXPERTS," that maybe they do not know best and maybe they do not have all the answers... maybe because they are not asking the right questions.

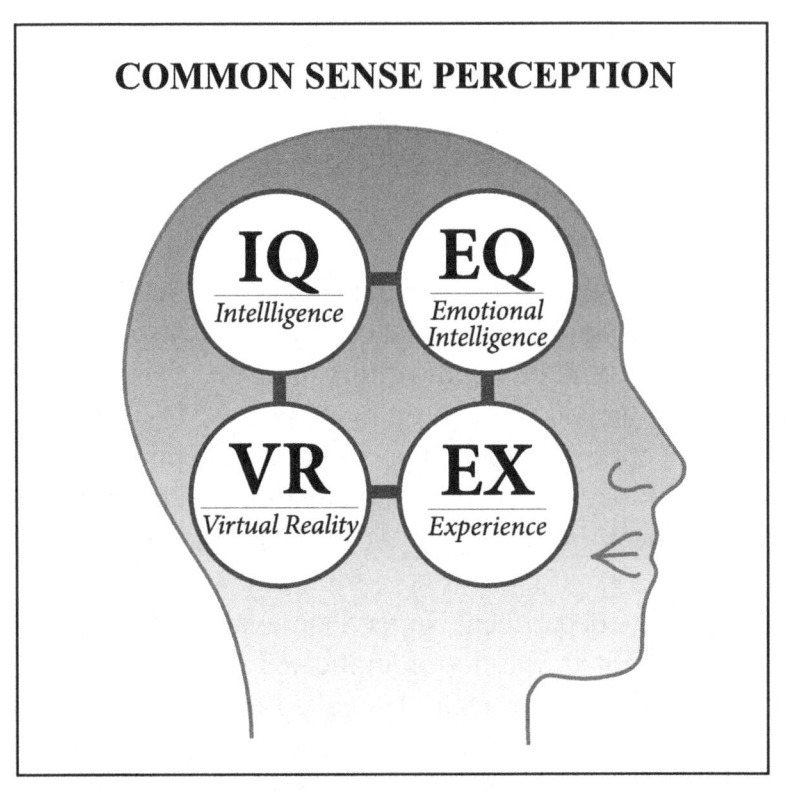

COMMON SENSE PERCEPTION

- **IQ** — *Intelligence*
- **EQ** — *Emotional Intelligence*
- **VR** — *Virtual Reality*
- **EX** — *Experience*

COMMON SENSE APPROACH:
A Different Perspective

How many times have you heard someone say, "That's just plain common sense," or read in the news, "Just use your common sense." Based on these comments, it seems that people assume that everyone has or should have what is known as "common sense" and that people are born with this innate, practical wisdom. As a matter of fact, a nationwide survey reveals that the majority of Americans believe that a high level of common sense can lead to healthier, happier and more successful lives.

So the question remains, why is common sense not common practice? We believe that common sense is a life skill that has to be developed. Only a part of our intelligence is inherent in our genes. However, we have the ability to develop and enhance the rest of our Common Sense Perception.

COMMON SENSE FORMULA = IQ + EQ + VR + EX

- IQ = Intelligence
  Einstein is an example of a genius who was extremely strong mathematically while being relatively weak verbally. Book smarts is another way to describe the analytical skills measured by IQ tests.

- EQ = Emotional Intelligence
  An individual's ability to manage him or herself as well as other relationships. It consists of four fundamental capabilities of self-awareness, self management, social awareness, and social skill. Employers now recognize that an individual with high EQ makes for good leadership potential and is a competitive edge in the marketplace.

- VR = Virtual Reality
  This is our label for learning that takes place through multiple learning styles such as visual learning, auditory learning, musical learning. For example, we learn from watching movies, by listening to recordings, by hearing stories, parables and fables read aloud to us. We learn about ethics and philosophy from proverbs and speeches or from mentors and the example of others. It's visualizing how to dance before we actually do the dance steps.

- EX = Experience
  We learn by actually doing the deed and succeeding so we know what works; or failing so we know what doesn't work. As Marilyn vos Savant, the woman with the highest IQ ever recorded said, "If you don't make mistakes, you probably don't know much."

An individual with a highly developed common sense perception has a critical balance of all four qualities and continues to develop them regularly. Which of these are you most comfortable with? Do you consider yourself more analytical or creative? Do you think you are more practical or theoretical?

The following story dramatically illustrates the difference between the two. Two students from a prestigious Ivy League school were camping in Yellowstone Park when they came across a grizzly bear. The first student, an academic whiz with a full scholarship, immediately calculates that the bear can reach them in exactly 19 seconds. "No way we can outrun him," he tells his companion who is putting on his running shoes. The other boy, who barely passed his entrance exams, says to his friend: "I don't need to outrun the bear. I just need to outrun you."

As a follow up on that thought, practical intelligence versus intellectual intelligence, did you know that scientists involved in the creation of Artificial Intelligence (AI) are at a loss when it comes to instilling common sense reasoning into it's robotic computers. The reason is the difficulty of programming emotional intelligence into their systems.

Question: In an emergency, which doctor would you choose to help your child ?
1. Dr. with 10 degrees, 10 honorary titles, published 10 books, no patients.
2. Dr. with one degree, 10 years experience, multiple children patients.

UNCOMMON SENSE
To reiterate:
Common Sense is not inherited
Common Sense must be learned.
Common Sense can be taught.
Common Sense comes from experience.

"The fault lies not with the mob, who demands nonsense, but with those who do not know how to produce anything else."
– Miguel de Cervantes Saavedra

Twelve Common Sense Principles *for Living*

1. Every day is a new beginning.
2. The first step is the most difficult.
3. If you never try, you will never succeed.
4. Things are not always what they seem.
5. Be ready when opportunity knocks.
6. You can be anything you want, but not everything.
7. If you're sure you're right, stay the course.
8. Turn life's challenges to your advantage.
9. Communication is the key.
10. Join forces for a greater cause.
11. Do the right thing right.
12. Honor the golden rule.

THE CIRCLE OF INFLUENCE

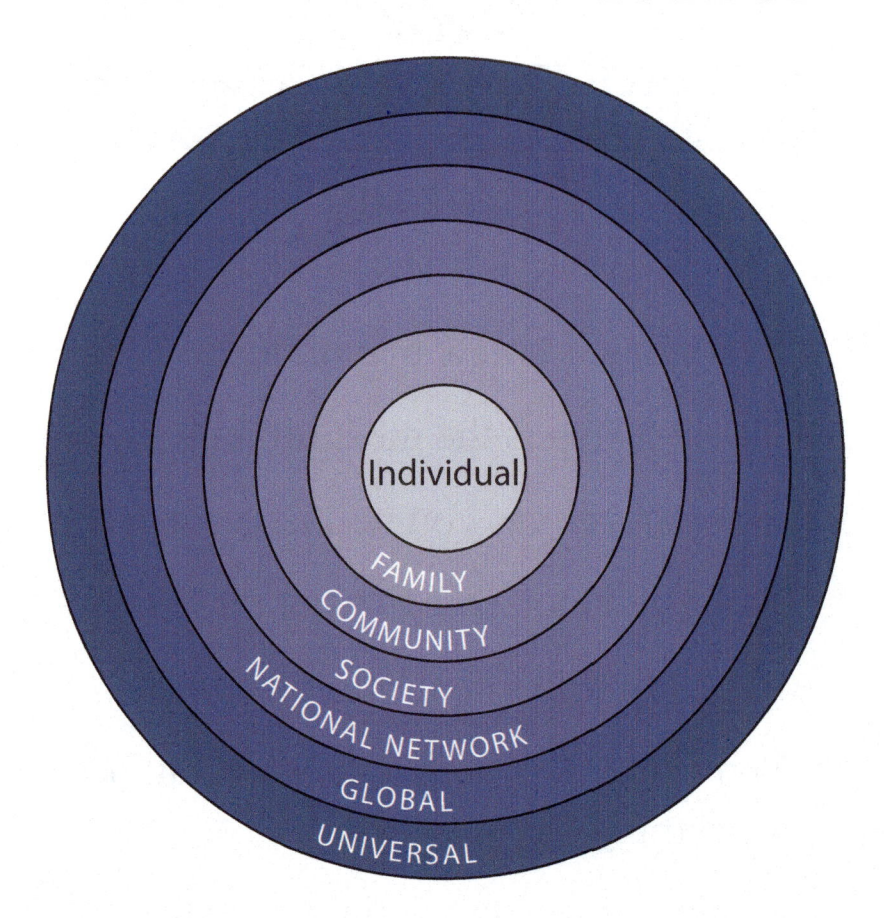

- Individual
- FAMILY
- COMMUNITY
- SOCIETY
- NATIONAL NETWORK
- GLOBAL
- UNIVERSAL

Circle of Influence

Relying on our common sense perception, we conclude that if we want people to grow up to be self-sufficient, contributing members of society then we need to teach them that responsibility begins with the individual. Once the individual is able to take care of himself/herself, then he is able to help others in the family. As soon as the family is able to take care of their survival and safety needs, then they are able to help their neighbors. This circle keeps expanding outward in a continuing cycle of helping hands.

This is the same process employers should follow in helping our community. Start with your own workplace then expand to the next neighborhood and community with best practices.

Cycle of Generations

Our goal is to provide a safe and nurturing haven for our families. We can do this so much more effectively when each generation shares in the task. Children and grandparents can create a bond that can keep a family together through the worst of disasters and the cruelest of tragedies. If each generation does its part, contributing their own talents and skills, then everyone benefits.

See illustration of Cycle of Generations.

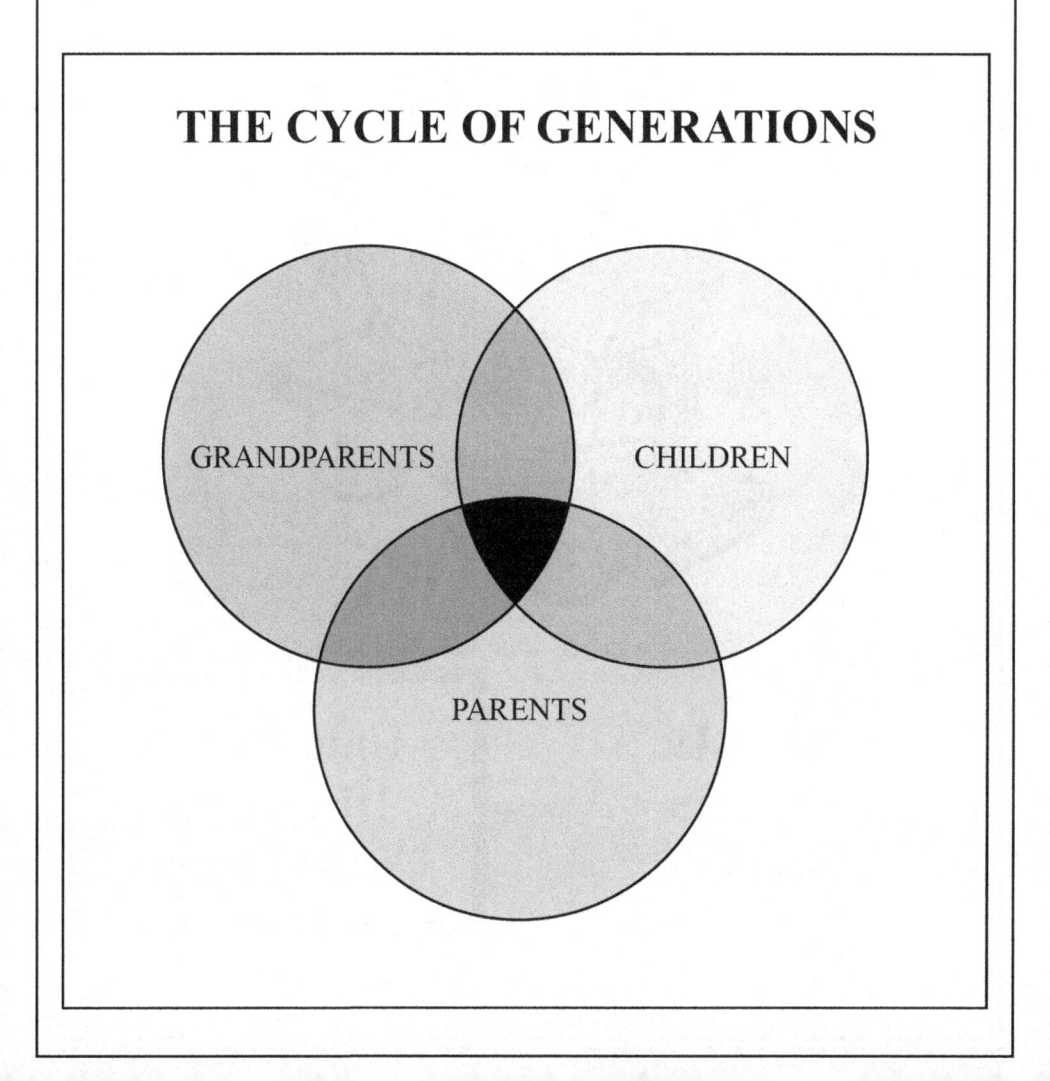

THE CYCLE OF GENERATIONS

GRANDPARENTS　　CHILDREN

PARENTS

Betrayed

| Active Shooters Violence | School Yard Bullies Cyber Bullying |

| COVD 19 Lockouts Mandates | Unintended Disastrous Consequences |

PARENT INVOLVEMENT

Remember what seems like a lifetime ago, we were sent invitations to workshops and conferences at the schools regarding emergency plans for countering Bullying and Cyber Bullying among the student body. We were encouraged to talk to counselors, teachers and administrators. We were asked to participate in antibullying efforts to combat the spread of bullying through the technology every student held in the palm of his hand. Parent participation was encouraged.

Active Shooter Training was the next required training. Parents were again asked to help prepare their children for the sometimes traumatic drills for every class. Board meetings were held to discuss how best to install new barriers on the outside of the school buildings. Parent input on what security system would be best to monitor the interior of the campus. Again, parents were advised and encouraged to submit their comments and suggestions.

BETRAYED

Is it any wonder then, that parents and grandparents felt betrayed when so many of our neighborhood schools just shut down and literally locked us out. There were no Parent-Teacher meetings to discuss options."

The parking lots were gated. Entrances to indoor facilities were chained. Access to outdoor facilities were blocked. Calls were not returned. Voicemail boxes were full.

ACCOUNTABILITY

Many schools stayed open.
Many schools chose to shut down.
Many schools were told to shut down by their local or state agencies
Many schools opted for a hybrid system.

WHAT DID YOUR NEIGHBORHOOD SCHOOL DO?

RECKONING

The usual management term used to evaluate the response to an emergency is "post-assessment." After two years plus of our reaction, response and treatment of the pandemic in our schools, I believe the more appropriate term is the one I am using here "RECKONING."

Reckoning signifies not just an evaluation, it clearly suggests a "Price to Pay."

PRICE TO PAY

Preliminary reports are now substantiating our worst fears. The repercussions of imposing lockouts, at home instruction, mask mandates and one way only approaches will be felt for years to come.

DYA : DO YOU AGREE?

Every child is unique, so every one of our children's health, mental and safety treatment should also be unique.

UNINTENDED CONSEQUENCES

Many of our schools mandated draconian rules with no exceptions and cited emergency powers. So why did we act surprised when we were faced with the following unintended consequences on our student population on every level Kindergarten through College.

- Bullycide
- Drug Overdose
- Mental Illness
- High School Drop-outs
- Domestic Violence
- Divorce
- Decrease in math and reading scores
- Increase in emotional needs
- Depression

> "What do you get when you mix science with politics?"

POLITICAL SCIENCE

> "What do you get when you mix philosophy with science?"

COMMON SENSE

ZOOM WORLD

Would it surprise you to know that many teachers were blindsided by the ramifications of the Lockouts. Some of our schools opted for a hybrid system so that some students would be on campus and others would participate in the day's lessons via ZOOM.

Ironically, it was not the students who had difficulty with the technology of using Zoom, it was the teachers and the parents who were asked to monitor their kids on the platform.

PULLING BACK THE CURTAIN

For the very first time because of a confluence of unforeseen circumstances, parents had the opportunity to witness first hand their children's teachers in action on the computer laptop. Many parents, of course, sat in on their children activities in elementary school but never had a chance to do so for their older kids. What they witnessed was sometimes stunning, sometimes shocking.

Many parents were impressed by the professionalism of so many instructors who could handle teaching 15 children in the classroom while at the same time interacting with another 30 students who were participating from their homes.

On the other hand, many parents were taken aback by the lack of training their children and teachers were given on how to use the Zoom platform and were frustrated in their attempts to help, often because of equipment failure on the schools part, or procedural shortcomings on their own. Many parents found themselves basically home schooling their children without the proper guidance in the technology.

SECRETS EXPOSED

Most disturbing was the incriminating evidence piling up regarding the content. Subject matter did not seem to match the school's purported curriculum on file for the grade level in question. Even more surprising was the attitude from the school staff that students should not tell their parents what was happening in the classrooms. At times, students were asked to keep information from their parents.

Helicopter Perspective

HELICOPTER VIEW

To clarify our comments regarding schools. We usually recommend that people make sure to take the Helicopter View before forming any opinions outside of their own personal observations.

First of all, every school campus is unique. Therefore every school's policies and curriculum must be unique:

- Unique to the student body, enrollment, gifts and potential;
- Unique to the faculty and staff with their talents and capabilities;
- Unique to the school campus grounds, buildings, utilities;
- Unique to the location with its benefits and hazards;
- Unique to the community and its resources.

Taking the Helicopter view reminds us that what is going on around the country where the news centers are located, do not necessarily reflect on what is happening in our own neighborhood school. This is the reason we recommend focusing on what we can control.

Develop the background you need to ask the difficult questions. Develop the priorities to help you find the answers to the challenges facing your school.

"You've got to have a plan of action, You have to stay focused on the things you can control, and don't get discouraged or distracted by the things you cannot control."

– Yankee Bernie Williams

Parents and Grandparents must love, protect, nurture and guide their children. Schools should help them by providing the resources, personnel, knowledge and activities to develop their skills, talents and intelligence to the best of their ability.

FOCUS

FOCUS ON
WHAT YOU CAN CONTROL!

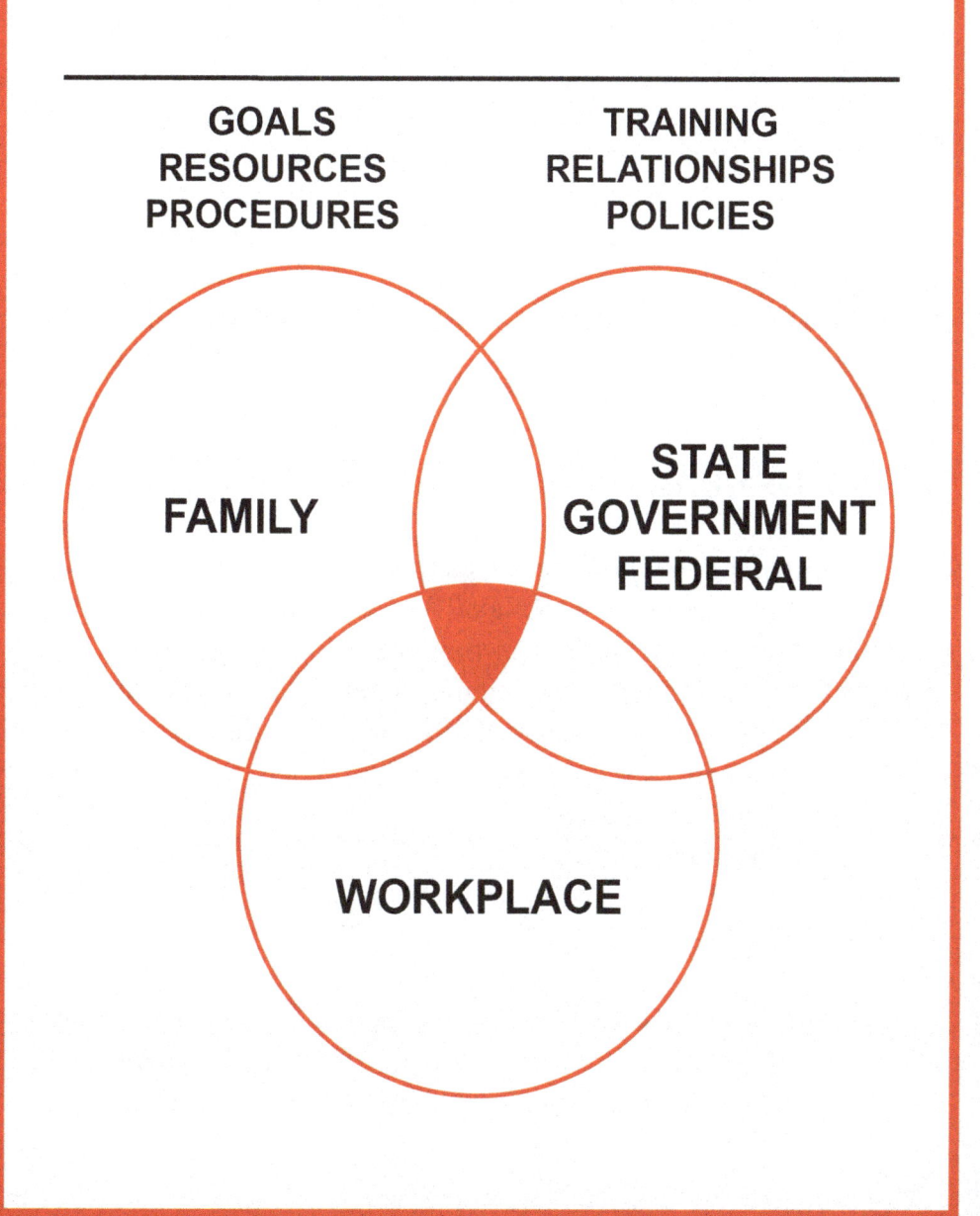

GOALS
RESOURCES
PROCEDURES

TRAINING
RELATIONSHIPS
POLICIES

FAMILY

STATE
GOVERNMENT
FEDERAL

WORKPLACE

WORKING TOGETHER

Pointing fingers and blaming others will not help find the solutions we need to improve the situation many of our schools find themselves facing in the post, pandemic divide. The lack of accountability is a problem which has caused the epidemic of excuses running rampant in our organizations from top to bottom.

School boards, Administration, Principals, teachers, staff, coaches, counselors, vendors, contractors, all have something to contribute. In order to find the solutions, everyone must take on the personal accountability of critically evaluating what went wrong during the pandemic and accepting the responsibility to make the changes needed to move forward so that our mistakes are not repeated.

The goal and the vision should be "How can we improve?" "How can I make a difference?" "What can we do better so this crisis doesn't happen again?"

RULE OF BENJAMIN

A practical method for establishing accountability and identifying priorities is the Rule of Benjamin. Using this tool and putting it into daily action can produce astonishing results. Put down every reason why a decision is beneficial or detrimental. In simpler terms, Every action, decision or policy should be based on these two considerations only:
1. Does it help our children?
2. Does it hurt our children?

ADVICE TO PARENTS

If we follow the Rule of Benjamin, hopefully we can get back on track. Forget about what we did in 2020 (Mask Them) and 2021 (Jab Them) Let's do the best thing in 2022 (Free Them).

The Rule of Benjamin

Pro

1. _____
2. _____
3. _____
4. _____
5. _____
6. _____
7. _____
8. _____
9. _____
10. _____

Con

1. _____
2. _____
3. _____
4. _____
5. _____
6. _____
7. _____
8. _____
9. _____
10. _____

1. List all items you can think of in both columns.

2. Ponder, analyze and apply a weight to each item.

3. Remove items from each column with the same weight.

Advice To Parents
How Times Change!

1910	Spank them!
1920	Deprive them!
1930	Ignore them!
1940	Reason with them!
1950	Love them!
1960	Spank them lovingly
1970	To heck with them!
1980	Esteem them!
1990	Embrace them!
2000	Empower them!
2010	Email them!
2015	Hover over them!
2016	Text them!
2017	Twitter them!
2018	Tik Tok them!
2019	Hide them!
2020	Mask them!
2021	Jab them!
2022	**FREE them!**

Note: An anonymous "Advice to Parents" from 1920-1970 could usually be found on the bulletin boards of any school teacher's lounge. We've updated the list.

THE SOUND OF SILENCE

Have we become desensitized to the idiocy going on all around us? Are we no longer able to raise our voice against the senseless cruelty and insanity.

"in the naked light I saw
Ten thousand people, maybe more
People talking without speaking
People hearing without listening
People writing songs that voices never share
And no one dared
Disturb the sound of silence

— Paul Simon

Are we so terrified of being canceled and not being accepted that we dare not raise the obvious questions that we should?

As parents and grandparents we must ask these questions.

Why did we lock out our children from their home away from home for two years? Why did we force them to cover their faces and take away the smiles of their friends and teachers?

"Because I said so?" is no longer good enough, no matter who is in charge. The answers must contain specific, evidence based reasons with details from all perspectives not just an opinion of one.

If we stay silent, we are permitting all that went wrong in our schools. We must stand up and accept the wake-up siren.

" Silence is the enemy of Truth."

> It takes a great deal of courage to stand alone, even if you believe in something very strongly.

– 12 Angry Men

PART 2

COMMUNICATION IS KEY

❝The single biggest problem in communication, is the illusion that it has taken place.❞

– George Bernard Shaw

" Men often hate each other because they fear each other; they fear each other because they don't know each other; they don't know each other because they can not communicate; they can not communicate because they are separated. "

— *"Stride Toward Freedom,"* 1958

WHY IS COMMUNICATION SO IMPORTANT?

Effective Communication is required for a society to function properly. Every facet of our daily lives depend on it.

Miscommunication can easily lead to misunderstanding. Misunderstanding can lead to a variety of consequences, none of them pleasant in the best case scenario, to devastating life or death results in the worst case scenario.

On a personal level, it could lead to broken relationships ultimately resulting in divorce or legal entanglements. On the business level, it could result in loss of income, loss of investment, bankruptcy. On the political level, misunderstanding can be the cause of escalating tensions which puts everyone in danger.

COMMUNICATION 101

THE BASIC ELEMENTS

The basic requirements for communication are:

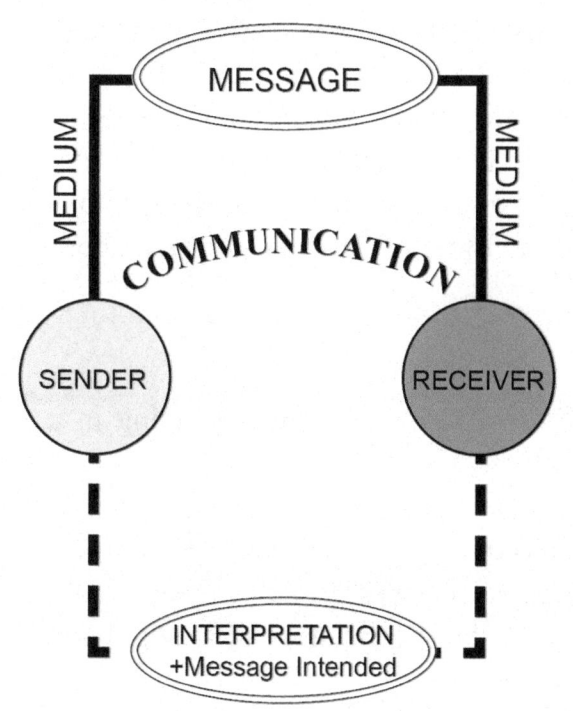

a sender
a reciever
a message
a medium
an interpretation

If the message received is interpreted in the same way the message was intended, then the communication has been executed effectively. If the message is not interpreted correctly, then there is a "miscommunication."

HOW TO COMPLETE A VALID COMMUNICATION

Answer the prime questions to determine the process.

WHO is the SENDER? WHO is the RECEIVER?
WHOSE is the MESSAGE?
WHAT is the MESSAGE?
WHERE is the SENDER? WHERE is the RECEIVER?
WHEN is the MESSAGE being sent?
WHY is the MESSAGE being sent?
WHICH is the MEDIUM used?
HOW is the MESSAGE sent? HOW is the MESSAGE received?

THE FOUR CATEGORIES OF COMMUNICATION

Time dictates the types of Communication we use at a particular moment in time. Listed in the order of time priorities.

1. Emergency Communication: Time Sensitive Warnings
Under emergency conditions, time is critical and any delay may result in loss of life. It is imperative that action be taken as soon as possible. The message must be clear, simple and direct. Use any and all resources available. Anyone who can help or bring help is the intended receiver. Leave no room for error in interpretation.

Examples:

- An elderly man suffers a heart attack while dining in a restaurant
- You are on your cell phone when you see a pedestrian hit
- Code Adam is announced over the PA system at Wal*Mart
- A woman is screaming "Help" as she's forced into a car
- Smoke is coming out of the second story of a neighbor's house

2. Ordinary Communication: Real Time News

We are bombarded by so much data every day that we are in danger of overload –and not enough time. The solution is to focus on our priorities and reserve those special moments with our families and loved ones.

Examples:

- Conversations with spouse, children, friends and pets
- Daily newspapers, magazines, talk radio, television news
- Meetings with co-workers, colleagues and associates
- Greetings to customers, clients, acquaintances, strangers
- Conferences with the boss, kid's teachers, neighbors
- Social activities with relatives and friends
- Gatherings at church, community associations, political groups

3. Reserved Communication: Time Delayed Lessons

We listen and go through the motions but we don't really understand the importance of these lessons until that "Aha" moment when we are forced to apply what we have learned.

Examples:

- Parents serving as role models on how to raise a family...
- Coach talking about the importance of physical fitness...
- Teacher introducing life skills in finance, cooking, carpentry
- Nurse explaining the harmful effect of smoking...
- Instructor demonstrating CPR and First Aid...
- Manager explaining how to handle difficult customers...
- Police promoting the value of Neighborhood Watch...

4. Enduring Communication: Timeless Principles

Universal truths are passed down to us from the scriptures of Christianity, Judaism, Islam, Hinduism, Confucianism, Buddhism, and others, including the wisdom of the ages taught by the great philosophers...

Examples:

- The Golden Rule
- Love Thy Neighbor
- Honor Thy Father and Mother
- Judge Not
- Speak Truth
- Seek and Ye Shall Find
- Respect all people
- Be Kind

THE SITUATION DETERMINES THE SOLUTION

THE TIME FACTOR

People have always been creative in developing methods to send a message from one point to another. The sounds of beating drums, the blowing of a conch shell, smoke signals from a mountain top, whistles in a forest, message in a bottle, bon fires, passenger pigeons, couriers in wagons, mail by pony express, all served a purpose.

Eventually the advance of time and progress introduced morse code, the telegraph, and the telephone which in short time evolved into pagers, mobile phones, fax machines, emails and 24/7 cable news. Once the internet took over, communication exploded into text and social media platforms including streaming services which dominate the marketplace.

THE CHALLENGES

What benefits technology provided us in "speed," it took away from us in accuracy. Time and again, effective communication from sender to receiver breaks down for one reason or another.

PROPOSITION

1. If the original message is altered by the medium, will the receiver be able to interpret the meaning correctly?
2. If the original message is delayed by the medium, will the receiver be able to trust the accuracy of the message?
3. If the message is blocked by the medium, will the receiver ever get the message?

ANSWER: NO, NO, and NO.

OUR HOMEWORK

Gone are the days when, as grandparents, all we had to worry about was trying to help the grandkids with their homework assignments like solving problems with the "new" math methods.

Today we have our own homework assignment. We have to be concerned about the policies our schools are executing.

Are the school boards and administration being open and honest about programs that affect our children? Are they doing what is best for our children?

From personal experience, many of our schools are doing exactly what they promised in their public statements. Some are not.

What is your neighborhood school doing? How can we help? Find the TRUTH.

WHAT IS TRUTH?

This is certainly one of the most important questions one can ask. The answer will certainly determine what one believes, what one values, whom we trust, how we live. To be honest, finding the truth is one of the most essential requirements we are tasked with accomplishing. Once we find it, we need to communicate it. Unfortunately, we are faced with so many obstacles in trying to find the truth. All self-inflicted.

FOUR BASIC APPROACHES TO THE TRUTH

- Objective Truth – what exists based on an accepted standard
- Subjective Truth – how one sees or experiences the world
- Normative Truth – what the collective agrees is true
- Complex Truth – grants the validity of all these truths and focuses on the most useful at a point in time.

FOUR THEORIES TO FINDING THE TRUTH

- Correspondence Theory – whatever corresponds to observable reality is true
- Coherence Theory – a statement is true if it follows logically and coherently from a set of propositions
- Consensus Theory – what is true, is whatever everyone agrees to is true
- Pragmatic Theory – what is true, is what is useful or beneficial to you.

TOOLS FOR CRITICAL THINKING

Do these approaches and theories cause more uncertainty in finding the answer? Each approach and/or each theory has strong arguments pro and con. Some are counter-intuitive, none are the complete answer. The search continues for the right answer but these are tools to help sort through all the obstacles ahead.

The Many Faces of Truth

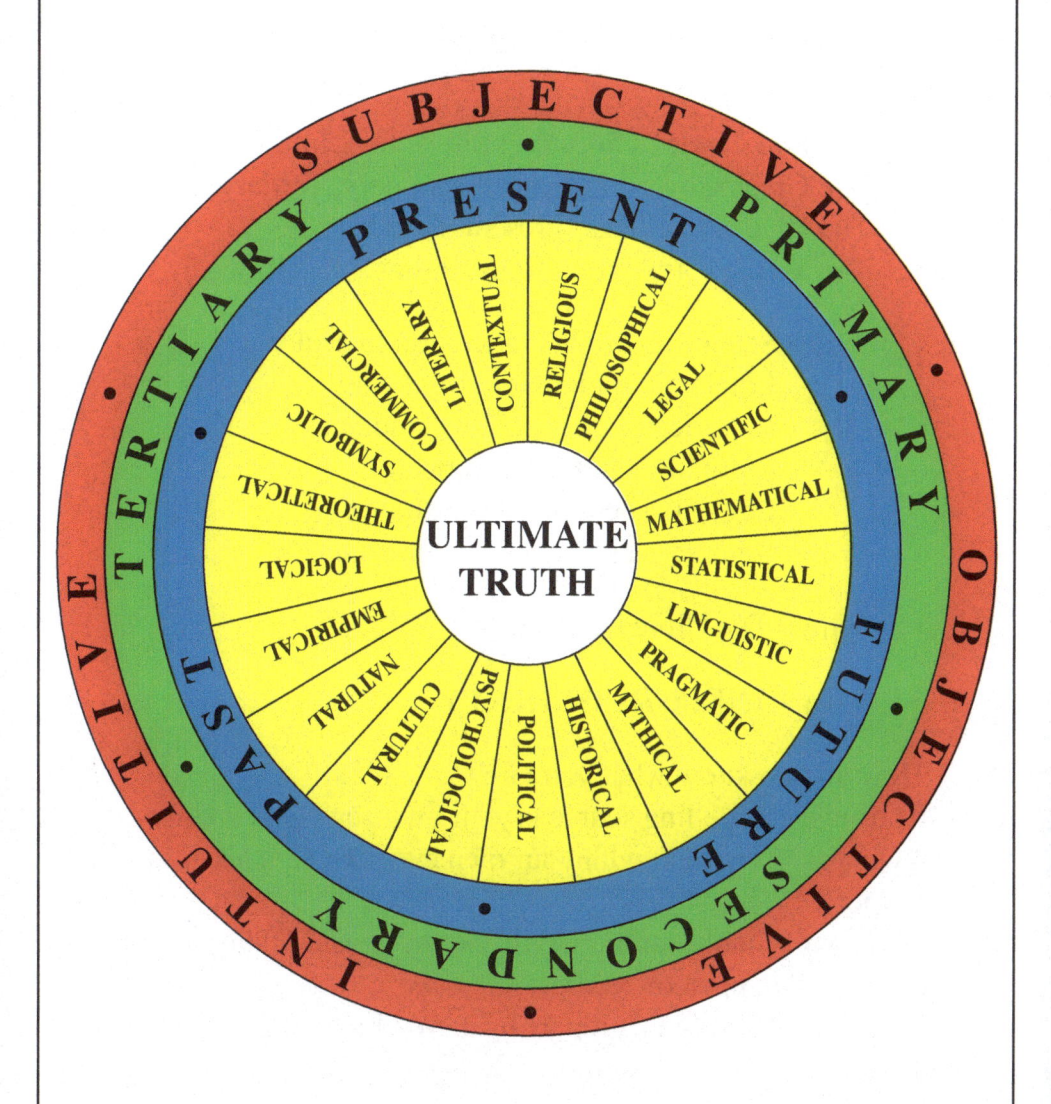

THE MANY FACES OF TRUTH

Review the Chart we have prepared to give you a better scope of understanding how complex it is to reach the Ultimate Truth.

SPIN THE WHEEL

Start with the outer circle and keep spinning inward until you reach the center.

- The Red Circle : Objective; Subjective; Intuitive
- The Green Circle : Primary; Secondary; Tertiary
- The Blue Circle: Past; Present; Future
- The Yellow Circle: Religious; Philosophical; Legal;

    Scientific; Mathematical; Statistical;
    Linguistic; Pragmatic; Mythical;
    Historical; Political; Psychological;
    Cultural; Natural; Empirical;
    Logical; Theoretical; Symbolic;
    Commercial; Literary; Contextual;

- White: The Ultimate Truth

BOTTOM LINE: CREDIBILITY

How do you know what you know?

The most compelling source is your own personal experience – you witnessed an event with your own eyes and ears because you were there.

The next reliable source would be video and audio evidence verified as untampered.

Third in reliability is a report by a credible witness you know and respect.

Fourth in line is a news source. But news in our current state of affairs uses anonymous sources, biased writers, opinionated panelists, and drama driven hosts.

Whom Do You Trust?

1. _____ a. Principal

2. _____ b. PTA

3. _____ c. Teacher

4. _____ d. Counselor

5. _____ e. Coach

6. _____ f. Business Manager

7. _____ g. Nurse

8. _____ h. Administrator

9. _____ i. School Board

10. _____ j. Colleague

11. _____ k. Department of Education

TRUST

Parents should have a trusted contact at the school their children attend. Look over the list provided here. Depending on the age level of your child, check all that apply.

Whom do you trust leads directly to Whom do you believe? Review the chart and fill in the answers starting at your top choice. There is no correct answer but for your information, you can compare your answers to the two charts, Global and USA Gallop Surveys which list the Most and the Least trusted professions. It does not surprise anyone to see the perennial winners of the Least trusted profession as Politicians and Bureaucrats.

"The Truth is like a Lion;
You don't have to defend it.
Let it loose:
It will defend itself."

– Augustine of Hippo

FOLLOW THE SCIENCE

What does "follow the science" mean ? If you turned on the television or listened to the media the past two years, you must have heard that phrase a thousand times or more. Here is the reason.

Looking at the chart listing Professions, " Scientists" tops all the other occupations as the most trustworthy – No. 1. Now consider who used that phrase over and over? Look at the Trustworthy list again. Go down to the bottom where Politicians and Bureaucrats are listed as the most untrustworthy – No. 1 & 2.

The use of "science," which most people find to be trustworthy, by politicians, who most people find untrustworthy, is not coincidental. It was intentionally done to trick us into believing everything they said or would say. After all, who can dispute science?

Whom Do You Believe?

1. _____
2. _____
3. _____
4. _____
5. _____
6. _____
7. _____
8. _____
9. _____
10. _____
11. _____

a. Celebrities
b. Politician
c. Local TV
d. Social Media like Facebook
e. Scientist - lab
f. National TV
g. T.V. Pundits
h. Your Doctor
i. News - Print
j. News - Cable
k. Government Agency

Global Trust in Professions from Ipsos 2019

Profession	% Trustworthy (1-2)	% Untrustworthy (4-5)
Scientists	60%	11%
Doctors	56%	14%
Teachers	52%	13%
Armed Forces	43%	19%
The Police	38%	28%
Ordinary men/women	37%	13%
Judges	32%	29%
Lawyers	25%	32%
Television news readers	24%	33%
Pollsters	23%	27%
Civil Servants	23%	33%
Business Leaders	22%	32%
Journalists	21%	38%
Clergy/Priests	21%	42%
Bankers	20%	41%
Advertising executives	13%	46%
Government ministers	12%	57%
Politician generally	9%	67%

Base: 19,587 online adults ages 16-74 across 23 countries

Least Trusted in U.S. / Gallop Data August 2021

Profession

Rank	Profession	Percentage
10	Judge	43%
9	Clergy	39%
8	Nursing Home Operators	36%
7	Bankers	29%
6	Journalists	28%
5	Lawyers	21%
4	Business Executives	17%
3	Advertising Practitioner	10%
2	Car Salespeople	8%
1	Members of Congress	8%

COMMUNICATION 102 :
Strategies for Creating Confusion

We know the Basic elements needed for communication to be accurate. What if, however, the intent of the sender was to intentionally sabotage accurate communication without the receiver knowing your intent?

The main strategies employed to prevent accurate communication are:

1. Present only a part of the story.
2. Mix up the time frame.
3. Dirty Tricks with the Facts
4. Lying

PARABLE OF THE BLIND MAN & THE ELEPHANT

Once upon a time, there were four blind men who gathered by the road-side every day, and talked about interesting topics. One of the friends brought up a strange creature his brother had told him about. The others said had often heard of elephants, but they had never seen one; of course, how could they?

It so happened one morning that an elephant was driven down the road where they stood. When they were told that the great beast was before them, they asked the driver to let him stop so that they might see him.

Naturally, they could not see him with their eyes; but they thought that by touching him they could learn just what kind of animal the elephant was.

The first one happened to put his hand on the elephant's side. "Well, well!" he said, "now I know all about this beast. He is exactly like a wall."

Parable of The Blind Man and The Elephant

The second felt only of the elephant's trunk. "My brother," he said, "you are mistaken. He is not at all like a wall. "Anybody who knows anything can see that this elephant is like a snake."

The third reached out his arms, and grasped one of the elephant's legs. "Oh, how blind you both are!" he said. "It is very plain to me that he is round and tall like a tree."

The fourth was a very tall man, and he reached up to take hold of the elephant's ear. "The blindest man ought to know that this beast is not like any of the things that you name," he said. "He is exactly like a huge fan."

"O foolish fellows!" they cried. They began to argue based on their own description and criticized one another "You surely have lost your senses. This elephant is not like what you proclaim. But any man with a iota of sense can see that he is exactly like what I said."

Then the driver of the elephant moved on, shaking his head after hearing the blind men quarreling about his beast. Each believed that he knew just how the animal looked; and each called the others crazy because they did not agree with him.

People who have eyes sometimes behave just as foolishly. Despite each blind man having an accurate observation of the part he inspected, his conclusion was so far from the actual reality of an elephant. Too often we are missing an important part or parts of the puzzle in order to reach a correct conclusion. The parable of the blind men and the elephant illustrates biases can blind us.

THE TIME PARADOX

Truth Delayed

Lessons of the Past

Past Grievances

REAL TIME

Future Corrections

Solutions for the Future

Truth Denied

Possible
Potential
Probable

Prepare
Practice
Prevent

NOW

THE TIME PARADOX

TIME is the missing element in a discussion on every important topic that affects our lives. The concept of Time is so difficult to explain so that is the reason people want to ignore it whenever they can get away with it.

Here are a few examples to keep in mind and raise your antenna:

- "The Science is Settled" : The very definition of the word science means a continual, active search for knowledge which means it can never be settled.
- "History Cannot Be Changed": Our recorded history changes everyday. Our knowledge base is increased with new discoveries in archeology, plus new scientific tools give us a better look into the past. What shouldn't change is an accurate portrayal of the events we are covering without a bias lens.

"We have to live today by what truth we can get today and be ready tomorrow to call it falsehood."

– William James

HOW DOES THE TIME FACTOR INTO OUR DAILY LIVES

- Why does it take so long (average about two years) for the Bureaucrats to verify news which was at first labeled untrustworthy?
- Why does it take so long before correct data on the unintentional effects of Covid 19 in our schools is released?
- Why does it take so long before parents and grandparents are given a voice in their neighborhood schools?

TRUTH DELAYED IS TRUTH DENIED.

> "TRUTH WILL OUT."
>
> – Shakespeare, Merchant of Venice

DIRTY TRICKS: Propaganda

Bullying and harassment don't simply go away at a certain age. Unfortunately, it is prevalent in countless aspects of society. Not only that but there are many weapons that are used to execute such bullying. Bullying is readily used in society today, especially with regard to propaganda Let's discuss the multifaceted weapon of trickery/deception used in propaganda techniques.

Firstly, stereotyping is weaponized in order to make others feel a certain way about a person or specific group of people. Usually, stereotypes have very negative connotations that can affect the well-being and safety of individuals or specific groups of people. In essence, stereotyping is giving a person or idea a negative label by using a memorable, contemptuous name.

This is typically used to make us reject and condemn a person or idea without examining what the label really means. For example, the words and phrases "treehugger", "environmentalist", or "special interest group" are all used to give negative labels. This is especially true when discussing mask and vaccine mandates in schools, branding some students as anti-maskers or anti-vaxxers.

Closely related to the stereotyping tactic is the unnecessary use of virtue words, also known as **glittering generalities**. This tactic uses words to deceive people into accepting and approving certain things or circumstances without properly examining the evidence. For example, words such as "natural", "democratic", "organic", "scientific", "ecological", and "sustainable" are given a positive connotation. This means that they are associated with good consequences.

Another method of manipulation that is not as commonly recognized, is called **deification**. This is a circumstance in which an idea is made to appear holy, sacred, or very special. However, any alternative or opposing points of view are given the appearance of treason or blasphemy. Examples include: "God-given right to…" or "Mother Earth."

There is also a form of bullying called **transfer**. This is when a symbol that carries respect, accompanies an idea or argument to make said argument appear more acceptable.

Examples: American Flag, University Seal, Medical Association Symbol, or something that resembles it.

Perhaps the most recognized tactic of bullying is **testimonials**. This is especially prevalent when it comes down to social media and ease of access to celebrities and other prominent figures. Testimonials occur when a respected individual such as a celebrity claims that something is good or bad. This technique is used to convince us without examining the facts more carefully. Illustrations of this can be vaccinations and mask mandates.

On the contrary, there is a manipulative tactic that is called, **plain folks**. This is often used by public speakers to convince an audience that an idea is good just because of similarities between the subject and the audience. Take for instance statements like: "This is the will of the people" or "Most decent Americans …" This form of deception basically encompasses the speaker telling a story about a family or people that are "just like you" for the sole purpose of reinforcing the speaker's point of view.

This is often confused with another form of bullying that is referred to as **bandwagon**. Similar to "plain folks", this tactic occurs when a certain speaker attempts to convince the general public to accept their point of view. The repercussion of not listening is the threat of missing out on something good. This technique, for example, is used in many forms of advertisement. For instance: "Act Now" campaigns or "What if you are the only one who doesn't have XYZ?"

Now, moving on to duality. Let's take **artificial dichotomy** for example. This is when someone tries to claim that there are only two sides to an issue. Furthermore, the argument is made that both sides must have an equal presentation in order to be evaluated. This, unfortunately, is black-and-white thinking. This type of thinking is used to manipulate people into believing that there is only one way to look at a certain issue, although there are numerous viewpoints to take into consideration.

Perhaps another popular form of manipulation is a technique known as a **hot potato**. This is an inflammatory and oftentimes untrue, statement that is intended to throw an opponent off guard or embarrass them. This is commonly seen in debates and political arenas. These are very bold statements intended to cause harm, such as "When will you pay the taxes you owe?"

Bullying does not always need to be aggressive behavior. In fact, many forms of bullying are mind games in which the victim is made to feel like something is their fault.

Take **stalling** or ignoring the question, for example. This technique avoids answering a specific question in hopes to get more time. This method is used so often, that many people do not realize it is a tactic of abuse. For example, when state and national mandates are enforced without reason. Think of some of the all too familiar phrases we hear: "More research is needed …" "A fact-finding committee is working on this issue…" "I am calling for an investigation on this failure.."

Another tactic bullies weaponize is something called **least-of-evils**. This method is used to justify an unpleasant point-of-view. This is used with both very serious and very minor circumstances. A more extravagant example would be: '"War is treacherous but appeasement leads to worse disasters"; while a milder example would be "Wearing masks is inconvenient, but not wearing masks leads to devastating effects."

Moving onto the **scapegoat** technique. This is often used with guilt-by-association in order to deflect scrutiny away from the issues. Simply put, it transfers blame from one person to another without discussing an issue's complexities and specifics. This is used most often in government, for example: "George W. Bush got us into Iraq" or "President Reagan caused the national debt". This can cause confusion about who is really responsible for what.

Another way these weaponized tactics confuse the general public is by utilizing something called **cause and effect mismatch**. This technique confuses the audience about the root of the cause and the reality of the effect. This is especially true in regard to healthcare. In fact, the causes of most phenomena are complex. For example, it is misleading to say only one of the following: "Tuberculosis is caused by bacteria." "Tuberculosis is caused by unregulated capitalism that creates poor working conditions." "Tuberculosis is caused by a lack of effective antibiotics." In essence, a speaker usually picks or chooses what is true and what is not.

That leads us to something called **distortion of data**, or cherry-picking, as some people call it. This specific technique is used to convince an audience of a particular idea by using selected information rather than the complete story. Take, for example, the statement: "A study was done that showed eating peanut butter causes liver cancer." However, the truth is that later, that particular study was shown to be flawed. Another example would be the statement: "Raising the speed limit to 65 mph resulted in many fewer traffic fatalities."

It is crucial that such statements be checked, along with how many people were driving before and after the change in speed limit. Fewer people may be driving after the speed limit change, even though the fatality rates may be higher, which leads to the overall result of fewer fatalities.

This is especially true when it comes to such critical matters like mandates regarding airborne illness. Dismissing such importance can lead to what is known as weak inference.

Weak inference or false cause happens when a judgment is made with insufficient evidence, especially when the conclusion does not necessarily follow from the evidence given.

In order to illustrate weak inference, take a look at the following example: Ducks and geese migrate south for the winter, therefore all waterfowl migrate south for the winter. Or, for instance: Most rich people vote Republican, therefore most people who vote Republican are rich. In this method of manipulation, correlation does not equal causation.

Similar to misinterpreting causation, we have something called **faulty analogy**. This is when a comparison is exaggerated and carried too far. This happens especially with regard to economics. Take the following sentence for example: "The economy is following the same path as right before the great depression, therefore we will experience a stock market crash soon!"

A single past circumstance does not always guarantee a similar future event. Using such a tactic is only to instill fear in others.

The next method of manipulation is actually an example of faulty analogy; it is called a "**slippery slope**." A slippery slope attempts to make an argument that a shift in one certain direction will continue to lead to extremes. We commonly see this illustrated in school systems, for example, "smoking marijuana will lead to future drug addiction." However, this is not necessarily true.

In fact, people in power often misuse statistics in order to support their exaggerated claims. The **misuse of statistics** is very often weaponized and used against the general public. Some examples include the presentation of average results, without the disclosure of the amount of variation regarding the averages. Usually, only a small portion of the full study is presented. This is also used as a scare tactic regarding crime rates, attempting to attack one's sense of personal safety. Take, for example, the statement: "3,400 more robberies occurred in our town last year, whereas other cities experienced an increase of less than one percent." No specifics are given.

Speaking of attack, another method of deception includes the **ad hominem attack**, which is sometimes referred to as deflection. This happens when someone attacks the messenger instead of confronting the message that was given. This is commonly witnessed in media, for example: Relying on socioeconomic status as a means to undermine an opposing individual's opinion – "You wouldn't understand since you have never had to struggle."

A **tu quoque attack** is another method of attack that is commonly seen. This typically occurs when someone responds to an opponent by accusing them of committing a logical fallacy or related propaganda technique. This is done instead of addressing the actual claim of the opponent's argument and/or their evidence. Again, many people tend to use fear as a propaganda technique, especially in regards to rules, regulations, mandates, and safety.

Not as commonly recognized as some of the others, but just as used is **preemptive framing**. This method can be interpreted as a solution looking for a problem, rather than an existing problem in need of a solution. This also includes mentioning an issue before other people get the chance to do so. As an example, see the following context: "The only reason the hacking of the poorly defended DNC (Democratic National Committee) is discussed, is that the loss by the Dems was so big that they were embarrassed." That statement is not an issue or a fact.

Lastly, we have the deceiving tactic of **diversion**. This is quite similar to stalling. This happens when a major issue arises that may be embarrassing or threatening to a certain person. Therefore, this person creates a diversion so that the subject of the matter can be avoided.

"Lying is the worst of all evils. Everything else that is diabolical, come from it."

– The Pianist

LYING

Lying is the worst of all the Dirty Tricks.
Many of the world's religions caution against lying:

Buddhism: Untruthfulness is not only to be avoided because it harms others, but also because it goes against the Buddhist ideal of finding the truth.

Christianity: There are six things the Lord hates, seven that are detestable to him: haughty eyes, a lying tongue, hands that shed innocent blood, a heart that devises wicked schemes, feet that are quick to rush into evil, a false witness who pours out lies and a person who stirs up conflict in the community.
Proverbs 6:16-19

Hinduism: "Truth always prevails"

Islam: "All the evils have been locked in a room and its key is lying."

Judaism: Deceiving others is strictly forbidden: "The Holy One, blessed be He, hates a person which says one thing with his mouth and another in his heart" [Babylonian Talmud]

Unfortunately, even with the proof of audio and video recordings, staring straight into the camera, under oath, in front of committees, in front of their colleagues...

Politicians still LIE
Bureaucrats still LIE

WATCH WHAT THEY DO, NOT WHAT THEY SAY

CALL TO ACTION FOR PARENTS & GRANDPARENTS

- Be Aware of what is going on in your child's school
- Be Prepared to stand up for what you believe
- Be Ready to demand accountability

PART 3

BULLIES

"Bullies want what they want when they want it. Bullies don't care whom they hurt. Bullies just want power to control you."

"Strong people stand up for themselves,

But the strongest people stand up for others."

THIS IS A BULLY FREE ZONE!

In 2010, with the incremental rise of student suicides caused by bullying, school districts across the country began to wake up to the very real harm caused by bullying. Approximately one-third of students are involved in peer bullying. Unbelievably, the highest rates are in elementary and middle school which continues into High School. Continual patterns of bullying leads to more aggression and contributes to the increase of school violence which often spirals into criminal acts in adulthood.

Targets of bullying suffer traumatic experiences causing depression, chronic anxiety, school absenteeism which in extreme cases can lead to bullycide or school shootings.

Parents and grandparents are demanding that schools become Bully Free Zones. Schools are required to provide a safe campus for their students. The increase in lawsuits is pressuring school districts to do something before they face their legal responsibility based on negligence, sexual or racial harassment.

THE BLAME GAME

We hear a lot about who is to blame. Parents tell us the schools are not doing their job and shirking their responsibility. Children tell us they are too afraid to get the adults involved and they don't want to be snitches. Teachers tell us their hands are tied by the administrators and the parents won't cooperate. Administrators are tired of trying different approaches with no success.

COMMON SENSE APPROACH

Playing the Blame Game will not solve the problem. To be honest, the only way to stop Bullying is to have all of the key players – from the cafeteria cook to the basketball coach to the principal to the classroom teacher to the bus driver to the concerned parent - become more aware, more proactive and more vigilant. The first step to take is to make sure we are all on the same page of understanding.

FACT or FICTION
DO YOU KNOW?

FACT or FICTION

☐	☐	1. Most acts of Bullying are never reported.
☐	☐	2. Bullying is a male behavior.
☐	☐	3. Bullying is a normal part of growing up.
☐	☐	4. Bystanders are always fearful of the Bully.
☐	☐	5. Bullycide is a term used to describe a suicide caused by bulling.
☐	☐	6. Bullying is always physical.
☐	☐	7. Parents will never accept being told their child is a bully.
☐	☐	8. Bullying happens only in large schools.
☐	☐	9. Girls do not bully.
☐	☐	10. There is no bullying in the elementary school.

FACT OR FICTION

If we do not know the facts about bullying, we might make the wrong decisions on how to approach the problem. Misinformation will lead us in the wrong direction of finding the solutions that are effective.

For the past 10 years we have teamed up with national anti-bullying organizations to introduce schools to the understanding that bullying is a problem that must be solved. The belief that bullying can never be solved is false.

One of the first things we do in our workshop is ask the important question.

What does bullying mean to you?

However you decide to describe your personal experience with bullying, the three basic elements involving bullying are:

- An imbalance of power

- An intent to harm

- A threat of further aggression

DO YOU KNOW QUIZ ?

The first step forward is to make sure we all understand what the issue we are discussing is about, we introduce our fact finding quiz. It is a way to make sure we distinguish between reality and rumor.

Read the statements in our Fact or Fiction Quiz. Don't be concerned if you don't know the answer. The purpose of the exercise is to highlight how much we don't know about bullying.

As parents and/or grandparents, we certainly want to do more to improve our children's school environments. We can work with the schools toward assuring a Bully Free Zone rather than placing blame. We can be involved in promoting respect for all of our kids. That is the message we need to send by helping to establish a Bully-free learning community.

FACT OR FICTION ANSWERS

FACT   1.   **Most acts of Bulling are never reported.**
Victims are reluctant to tell usually out of fear it will get worse.

FICTION 2.   **Bullying is a male behavior.**
Males are more likely to engage in physical acts like kicking, punching, screaming.
Females resort to gossip, shunning, cyber bullying.

FICTION 3.   **Bullying is a normal part of growing up.**
Aggression against a weaker victim is not natural and not to be tolerated.

FICTION 4.   **Bystanders are always fearful of the Bully.**
Some bystanders may fear the Bully. Others may encourage the behavior and Turn into henchmen.

FACT   5.   **Bullycide is a term used to describe a suicide caused by bullying.**
Suicide is the third-leading cause of death for Americans between the ages of 15-24. The term was coined by the authors of the book "Bullycide."

FICTION 6.   **Bullying is always physical.**
Verbal bullying, Social and Emotional bullying and the rise of Cyber bullying are even more frequent than physical or sexual bullying.

FACT   7.   **Parents will never accept being told their child is a bully.**
Parents are reluctant to think their child would behave in such a manner but in our experience, some parents are grateful to get the help from teachers and counselors.

FICTION 8.   **Bullying happens only in large schools.**
Research finds that actually students in smaller schools bullied more.

FICTION 9.   **Girls do not bully.**
Bullying is not gender exclusive. Manipulation, backstabbing, exclusion are parts of relationship bullying that girls engage in mire so than the boys.

FICTION 10.   **There is no bullying in the elementary school.**
Bullies are everywhere, from pre-kindergarten and beyond.

Best Practice to End BULLYING

All teachers and staff trained how to intervene to stop bullying	Parent and Guardian Workshops
Core Staff trained in Positive Strategies	Student Assemblies and Use of Technology

Key building blocks for a Bully-Free learning community

PROFILES OF THE KEY PLAYERS IN SCHOOL BULLYING

THE VICTIMS

A Victim is defined as someone who is repeatedly bullied. Victims are usually physically weaker, socially vulnerable and unable to have strong relationships with their peers. They tend to be insecure and react emotionally which only increases the bully events.

THE BULLY

Bullies take advantage of those they deem weak and easily controllable. Contrary to the typical image of a loner, Bullies are confident, strong and popular. They are usually leaders in the school through their roles in athletics, academics or other school activities.

THE HENCHMEN

These are usually friends or allies of the Bully. Henchmen usually will not act alone but once encouraged by the Bully they become more aggressive and eagerly join in the attack.

THE BYSTANDER

Bystanders are difficult to define as their motivations change. Sometimes they are passive and don't want to get involved. Sometimes they are fearful and don't want to be the next target. Often they don't know how to react and wait until they see what everybody else is doing. However, if they are friends of the victim and don't do anything to support their friend, the victim feels betrayed and makes it more difficult to trust anyone.

MULIPLE ROLES

The victim becomes the bully. Hurt and abused, children will lash out and attack others in the same way they were. This is why it is so important to view bullying situations in a comprehensive approach. Parents and educators must include all of the actions and circumstances that precede the actual aggressive events.

Profiles of Key Players in School Bullying

VICTIMS
OUR CHILDREN

BULLY

HENCHMEN

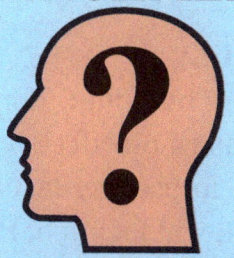

BYSTANDER

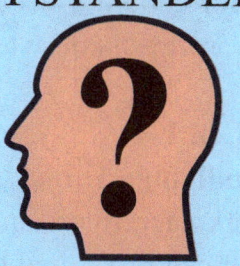

Which Role Are You?

TYPES OF WORPLACE BULLYING

- **I WANT TO SEE YOUR MANAGER BULLY**
  AKA Client bullying: Client bullying is often abusive and obnoxious, but will be defended by bullies because it is justified as services they are owed because they "paid" for it. **Examples are everywhere such as irate customers demanding a table without reservations, teachers assaulted by unruly students, guests demanding upgrades at a hotel, hospital workers threatened by their patients.**

- **THE OLD BOY BULLY**
  AKA Institutional bullying: Institutional bullying results when bullying becomes the accepted norm in the workplace. This can occur when one bully is always replaced by a new one (the first bully moves on to a new position). Over time, bullying becomes the norm, as employees become used to the fact that one old boy will replace another in a rotating game of musical chairs.

- **THE SUCK UP BULLY**
  AKA Prima Donna bullying: Some bullies want to be perceived as the best and most effective people in the workplace, and they are willing to use any tactics to undermine people who may perform better at their job. For example, an attention seeking bully might try to blackmail you into allowing them to take credit for certain aspects of your work, or they may insist that you are to blame when they make mistakes.

- **BY THE BOOK BULLY**
  AKA Regulation bullying: Through enforcing unnecessary or inappropriate workplace rules, an employer or employee in a position of power can make their target feel demeaned and powerless.

Bullying and the Hierarchy of Needs

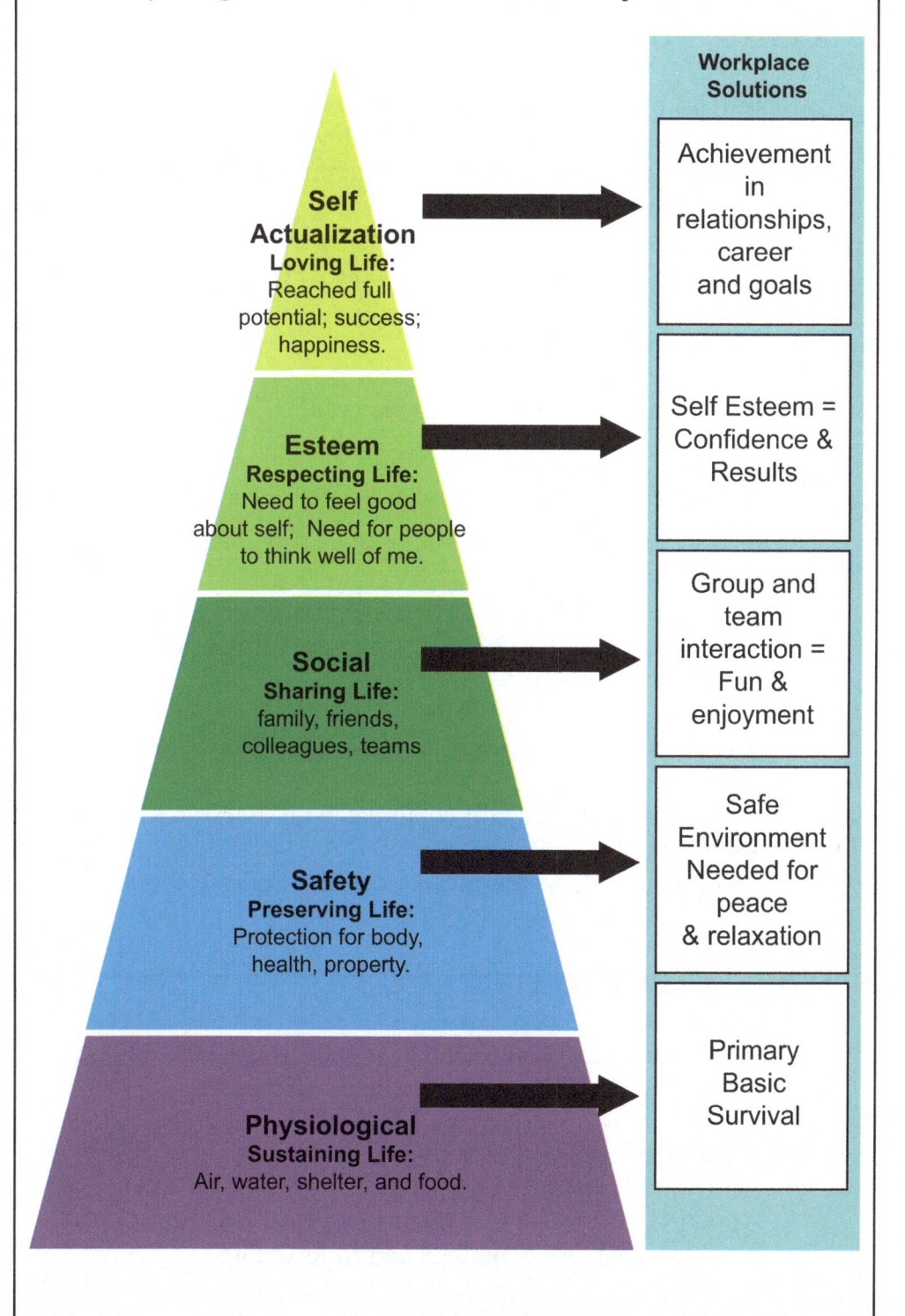

Self Actualization
Loving Life: Reached full potential; success; happiness.

Esteem
Respecting Life: Need to feel good about self; Need for people to think well of me.

Social
Sharing Life: family, friends, colleagues, teams

Safety
Preserving Life: Protection for body, health, property.

Physiological
Sustaining Life: Air, water, shelter, and food.

Workplace Solutions

- Achievement in relationships, career and goals
- Self Esteem = Confidence & Results
- Group and team interaction = Fun & enjoyment
- Safe Environment Needed for peace & relaxation
- Primary Basic Survival

BULLYING CONFRONTED HEAD ON

ANATOMY OF A BULLY'S MIND

Research by professionals in the fields of education, psychology, parent training and family development have added to the knowledge we have about the motivation of a bully's mind.

Child psychologists, behavioral health experts and parent educators trained to work with public, private and parochial school systems throughout the country have all contributed to the "Best Practices to End Bullying."

The two important takeaways are:
1. Recognizing the problem
2. We must do something to intervene

BULLYING IN SCHOOLS

Why is it so important that we create Bully Free Zones in schools?

The Department of Education and Secret Service offered these notable insights from their report "The Safe Schools Initiative," regarding Active Shooters.

- Almost all of the attackers (95 %) were former or current students at the school.
- 71% of attackers felt bullied, threatened, attacked or injured by others.
- More than half of the attacks occurred during the school day.

WORKPLACE BULLYING

Human Resources are proactive in setting up Anti-Bullying policies which are explicit in the company handbook

- Positive behaviors are reinforced
- The policy is publicized
- Surveys, data collection, written reports are emphasized
- Consequences are explained and followed up

Anatomy of a Bully's Mind
– What, Where When, Who, Why, How –

THE VICTIM TRIANGLE

```
          △
        DESIRE   ABILITY
         VICTIM
      OPPORTUNITY
```

Desire: The Bully has a need to gain power, control and purpose over others.

Ability: The Bully believes he has the ability to accomplish his goal. He plans and practices what to do and what not to do. He collects all the weapons, allies and tactics he needs. He practices. He never stops.

Opportunity: This is the crucial element between the Bully succeeding or even an attempt being made. The opportunity denied, prevents the act from occurring.

UNANSWERED QUESTIONS

WHAT IS...?

✦ *Justice without Wisdom?*

✦ *Success without Compassion?*

✦ *Marriage without Love?*

✦ *Freedom without Responsibility?*

✦ *Bureaucracy without Accountability?*

✦ *Government without Honesty?*

✦ *Power without Self-Control?*

— A. J. Lactaoen

WE NEED ANSWERS

Despite the progress we have made in confronting Bullying in the schools and in the workplace over the past decade, we have fallen far short in answering the serious questions that face our society.

It was in 1925 that Mahatma Gandi first published his list of what he called the "Seven Deadly Sins." His stark warning was that these are the things that will destroy us.

We focus on two on the list as it seems likely that because we ignored Gandi's warning, we allowed a new type of Bullying to creep into our society that we should have anticipated, but we did not.

WHAT IS

Science Without Humanity?

If science concentrates only on technology without consideration of the higher purposes of humanity, then we become prisoners of our own advances. The explosion of scientific discoveries is supposed to be a boon to solving the human condition. If the revolution of scientific experiment only adds to our problems, and the old injustices are still with us, then science can very well degenerate into becoming a foil rather than a solution.

The question behind the question becomes did Science save us from Covid 19 or did Science create Covid 19 in the first place?

WHAT IS

Politics Without Principle?

"We hold these Truths to be self-evident, that all Men are created equal, that they are endowed by their Creator with certain unalienable Rights, that among these are Life, Liberty, and the Pursuit of Happiness…'

If the value system of a society is aligned with correct principles, then the words of the Declaration hold meaning. In corrupt societies, there is no value to the words if there is no political will to stand by the principle of natural law.

The question behind the question is what does Science have to do with Politics?

PREVIEW OF COMING ATTRACTIONS

We indicated that there is a new type of Bullying festering in our communities. Again, we need to reemphasize the reason it was allowed to ripen in front of our eyes.

MORE UNANSWERED QUESTIONS

> **WHAT IS...** Power without Self-Control?
>
> **WHAT IS...** Government without Honesty?
>
> **WHAT IS...** Bureaucracy without Accountability?

These are just three of the ones we have listed. Our problem is not that we don't know the answers…yet…our problem is that we haven't even asked the questions.

What if we were to ask these unanswered questions of every politician running for office? What if we requested an answer from every one of our elected leaders? Would finding out what they really believe be more advantageous than listening to rehearsed Q&A posed by propagandists?

BUREAUCRACY WITHOUT ACCOUNTABILITY

Reflecting back on the whirlwind of the past two years, there have been many circumstances that we may not have understood. However, after persevering and gaining our footing, the unfathomable may begin to be digested. We can now dissect bureaucracy, accountability, integrity, and deficiency. Let's explore the ways in which the government's failed attempt at stabilizing the nation ultimately misused its powers.

Let's Breakdown Bureaucracy

It is a system of government wherein most cases, important decisions are made by state officials rather than elected representatives. What's more, 'bureaucracy' refers to both a body of non-elected officials and an administrative policy-making group.

Why Was The Crisis So Bad?

The COVID-19 crisis was a tragic blow to the country and its citizens in more ways than one. The physical and economic impact shook the nation to its core, all while the government's misuse of power added to its force.

Federal, state, and local governments responded to the crisis in such a way that influenced election rules and operations, political campaigns, the economy, schools, and more.

To combat the COVID-19 crisis, government officials were challenged to act in ways that are typically reserved for war, depressions, and natural disasters. The government took extreme measures to limit human costs and economic downturn. But, how?

Take, for example, shelter in place orders, mask mandates, and vaccine mandates. While these rules were seemingly put in place to benefit citizens, they soon began to have negative consequences.

How The Mandates Backfired

Some officials disobeyed their own mandates. Many government officials were seen traveling for vacation, hosting dinner parties and large gatherings, while others were forced to be at home.

When specific vaccine mandates came about, there were unfair exemptions granted to certain groups of people. While some working individuals risked their livelihood by opposing the vaccine, others were granted exemptions. Even certain government officials refused the vaccine, but they were able to keep their employment status.

There were two different sides to the story. In one circumstance, government officials and select individuals did not follow their own mandates. On the other hand, everyday hard-working people did not have a say in the matter and risked their jobs and social status. It even caused division among those who disagreed on wearing a mask and getting the vaccine.

How Did The Government Abuse Power?

The condition of democracy and human rights has greatly declined in countries worldwide. As a result, governments have engaged in abuses of power by silencing critics, and weakening important businesses, while abusing the systems of accountability needed to protect public health. In fact, in a recent survey, 27 percent of people reported government abuse of power as one of the major issues affected by the outbreak of COVID-19. There was also a lack of transparency in the government, allowing the population to be led blind. Not to mention the hypocrisy among government officials as many carried out their day-to-day leisurely activities.

Where is the accountability and integrity? Where is the model behavior of bureaucracy?

GOVERNMENT WITHOUT HONESTY

THE LESSON OF *"MISTER SMITH GOES TO WASHINGTON"*

Mr. Smith Goes to Washington is a classic 1939 American political comedy-drama film that depicts an idealistic young man who becomes appointed to the United States Senate. Consequently, he gains the mentorship of a prominent senator who is not as noble as his reputation boasts. This senator becomes involved in a scheme to discredit the newly appointed young man, who wants to build a boys' campsite–in place of a more lucrative project. However, this young man, Mr. Smith would not go down without a fight and he takes his case to the Senate floor.

Perhaps this iconic movie, though fiction, highlights similarities we see in society today–proven throughout history. This film was almost banned on several occasions simply because it touches on political corruption. The movie was denounced by Washington insiders who raged against these allegations of corruption in Washington. Unfortunately, this is no surprise since it's been happening since ancient times.

Take for example, how the news was suppressed in historical times. Ancient scribes often wrote the information down or spread any news by word of mouth. Therefore, merchants, sailors, and travelers brought the news back to their mainland and spread it from town to town. Messengers were often attacked and/or killed in order to prevent the spread of news, which is why written news was highly unreliable because it was often never delivered. And at the risk of unwanted information spreading, some citizens even took down the posted bulletins and destroyed the written information.

This type of behavior regarding the media carries over into this day and age–though not as extreme. Nevertheless, big media continues to control the narrative. Although, newsworthy stories of today differ dramatically from news stories covered in decades past. The internet has become a major news source for the most recent generations–especially when it comes to finding news on social platforms. The issue with these platforms is that many owners and chief executive officers of the publications or social media outlets can block user access altogether.

For quite some time now, there has been an obsession with media, along with its power to influence our thoughts and promote propaganda. Information is becoming misused, and misinformation is spreading much more quickly due to the instant nature of social media and online news.

Anyone who goes against the grain to weed out misinformation, in order to amplify true and important news stories, may very well be putting their futures and their well-being in jeopardy. This is because not only has the quality of news changed, but the punishment has also changed dramatically.

Studies show that we still, theoretically "shoot the messenger" when we receive information that doesn't appeal to us. For example, when we receive news we agree with–we like the messenger. When we are given less than favorable information–we dislike the messenger.

Not to mention forms of retaliation against the messenger such as verbal abuse, slander, threats, workplace termination, ostracization, and more. This discourages people from speaking up and speaking the truth. It is one of the most cunning ways that big media holds an influence on consumers. These circumstances illustrate that times have not changed, only the methods have.

Are we still as naïve as Jimmy Stewart was in his role as the patriotic Mr. Smith? Do we still believe that our elected officials are doing what they promised their constituents they would do when elected?

Will we teach our children to stand up to the bullies who control the streets and the news? Will we teach our children not to become cynical and give up the fight because you can't fight the powerful?

I hope so.

POWER WITHOUT SELF-CONTROL

"Power Corrupts. Absolute Power corrupts Absolutely."
– Lord Acton

When Absolute Power reigns supreme, then "consent of the governed," the idea that a government's legitimacy and moral right to use state power is justified is simply cast aside. In its place is the belief that no explanation is forthcoming, no questions are necessary, no criticism is tolerated, no disobedience is allowed.

People understand that difficult times demand difficult responses. But people also expect truthful answers. They also expect solutions that make sense. The benefit of the doubt only goes so far once demands are made that are harmful to our children and grandchildren. Then the demands of "Because I Said So," or "Do What I Say, Not What I Do," becomes the trigger to a resounding, defiant NO, We WON'T.

"All things are subject to interpretation whichever interpretation prevails at a given time is a function of power and not truth."
– Friedrich Nietzsche

Herein lies the ultimate power we have been subjected to in the past two years. The Bully has fashioned himself in his own image. The Bully controls the news, therefore he controls the interpretation, ergo he controls the story.

In the language of Myth, the storyteller is like a god. If the Bully is a god, then how can anyone defy him. If the Bully is a god, then whatever he says must be obeyed because he knows best. If the Bully is a god, then anyone who speaks ill of his decisions, is a blasphemer. If the Bully is a god, then we must obey all of his commands, we must perform all of his required rituals. If we do not, then we will suffer all of the punishments we deserve. We let the Bully create our Frankenstein. The Bully's name is…

COVID, THE GREAT, THE POWERFUL, THE ALMIGHTY

COVID
The Great and Powerful

Who is Behind the Mask?

THE CREATION MYTH
What a deliciously ingenious story line for the birthing of the Almighty Covid to be born in a cave. The symbolic narrative describing the humble beginnings of the pandemic that brought mankind to its knees in fear and utter obedience to the pronouncements of Covid's henchmen. The imagery had to be scary, dark, creepy just like it's host, the mutant bat creature that abhors the light. As in all creation myths, there is only one official version. All other versions like the ridiculous claim of unethical scientists creating biological weapons of war in secret must be banned.

ALL POWERFUL
COVID the Almighty demonstrated that it was the most powerful god of all. An invisible, airborne virus was more destructive than nuclear bombs, category 5 hurricanes, earthquakes, tornadoes, and a plethora of other everyday disasters. It was capable of overtaking the world and shutting it down, country by country. However, no one could ever see it coming. There were no warning signs, almost as if it were lurking around the corner hiding ironically–behind a mask.

HENCHMEN
In most world religions, there are leaders who provide guidance for their followers in life's day to day activities. These include prophets, rabbis, priests, monks, imams, judges. They often help the general public uphold themselves to a certain moral standard. However, the Almighty Covid relies only on politicians and bureaucrats to demand obedience to rules and regulations.

RULES AND REGULATIONS
"Do what we say, not what we do." Bureaucrats under the Almighty Covid have free reign to make up regulations on the spot using the Executive Emergency Order ploy. Due Process and Rules for extending Emergency Powers be damned.

DRESS CODE FOR THE CAMERA
COVID the Almighty demanded appropriate attire in front of the camera, optional behind the camera. For example, masks, gloves, face shields, etc. were mandatory in order to be welcomed into certain places or there would otherwise be a risk of rejection and ostracization. While some wear the attire to protect their health, others have simply adopted such behavior as normal. Or are they simply dressing to impress.

RITUALS
Similarly, rituals have been adopted as a sense of normalcy. Needing badges, identification, and passwords for an activity that previously did not require such things, is somewhat haunting. It's almost as if a secret password is now needed to access basic everyday activities.

ATTENDANCE
Regular attendance at certain services is a must for some beliefs. However, now more than ever parishioners are forced to watch their services via television or the internet. It has become almost like a ritual. Service goers are somewhat isolated, forced to enjoy their service from a screen.

INITIATION
Some beliefs require the traditions of initiation…Covid the Almighty requires a jab by needles. In order to go back to normal, many people are required to receive as many doses of the injection as Covid's henchmen demand.

REBUKE
It seems that those who decline the initiation are in essence deemed as unbelievers. These unbelievers are then punished by banishment, lockdowns, and shunning. Taking it a step further, they are publicly humiliated and sometimes even have their titles and statuses revoked. How much can one agree or disagree before this shunning occurs? Who is the judge who orders such repercussions? Is it again–some faceless bureaucrat hiding behind the mask that must be worn? Or is it some wizard hiding behind a curtain?

SALVATION
Our work in the development of anti-bullying programs in schools and in the workplace have given us the tools to break the hypnotic trance Covid the Almighty has captured our minds and wills.

1. We must be aware of the problem

2. We must intervene

ALMIGHTY COVID'S HENCHMEN – THE BETRAYAL

In order to foster an effective anti-bullying program in our schools and in our workplace, we have learned through experience that Best Practices requires the participation of all stakeholders. For this reason it is especially disheartening to see some school administrations and corporate boards who are against the tactics of BULLIES, turn into the unintended allies of the Almighty Covid. Rather than calling on all stakeholders to participate, they have usurped the authority we allowed them to use by fiat. Instead of finding the best way forward, they have turned limited emergency powers to unlimited status and corrupted the meaning of "consent of the governed. "

THE WEAPONS OF THE ULTRA BULLY

FEAR

Death, Dying alone, Dying in Pain, Dying a slow painful death, Dying w/o your loved ones at your side, Dying w/o your Priest or Rabbi or Religious Counselor, Dying in a hospital w/o your beloved pet…

Killing, Killing your spouse, Killing your loved ones, Killing your family, Killing your neighbors, Killing your friends, Killing strangers…

Yes, this is what will happen, you face the risk of Dying or Killing if you don't do exactly what they say!

BRIBERY

Of course, some people are not afraid, they don't react to irrational fear, they can't be scared into doing. But they can be bought. So, BULLY SAYS let's offer these types of characters a chance at winning a lottery. Maybe a $100,000 ? Maybe a car? Maybe a trip for 2? And don't forget the low ballers, maybe we can get them for a couple of free Big Macs?

SHUNNING & SHAMING

Some people can't be scared. Some people can't be bought. This is when the Bully resorts to the old saying "Guilt is good." These personalities respond to the Bully tactic of accusations: " you're selfish," "you are making things harder," "you are not thinking of your parents," you…you…you are bad.

You are so bad, you will need to be isolated. You might have to be confined to home assignment. Or you will have to do quarantine or lockdown voluntarily.

PUNISHMENT

This is a tactic that is frowned upon by human resource people in most organizations, and certainly by counselors in schools. As a matter of fact, this tactic, sometimes crossing over to retaliation, would be considered illegal in ordinary circumstances.

But not now. This is an emergency. So if you don't do what the Bully's Henchmen say, no exemptions, you will be terminated, fined, put on involuntary leave, removed, demoted, shunned, forgotten.

This is the BULLY GOSPEL.

"Power is of two kinds. One is obtained by the fear of punishment and the other by acts of love. Power based on love is a thousand times more effective and permanent then the one derived from fear of punishment."
– Mahatma Gandhi

"First they ignore you, then they laugh at you, then they fight you, then you win."
– Mahatma Gandhi

PART 4

LOCKOUTS & MANDATES

> "I will remember that there is art to medicine as well as science, and that warmth, sympathy, and understanding may outweigh the surgeon's knife or the chemist's drug."

– Hippocratic Oath Modern Louis Lasagna

THE BUREAUCRATIC WAY

"Stay away from bureaucrats, they have a problem for every solution."

COVID – 19 was introduced to an unsuspecting populace as an unknown invisible virus that could kill you. The media jumped on the chaos which only increased the FEAR. Instead of trying to calm people, the bureaucrats hit the panic button.

THE FOUR FEARS

Fear of the Unknown

The explanation on what the new virus is and where it came from was confusing at best. misleading definitely.

Reports from around the globe pointed to China as the original location. Not many seem to dispute that now.

The media ran with the imagery of bats in caves spreading the virus by infecting exotic animals slaughtered and sold at meat markets in densely populated restaurant areas in Chinatown.

Contrast that with the alternate explanation that the virus was created in a lab.

Either explanation sent shivers down the normal person who depends on our health professionals to take care of us and our families.

Result: PANIC

Fear of Loss

The cruelest mandates of all were that we needed to separate families. People were convinced that they would be guilty of infecting their loved ones. Thus began the inhumane treatment of people condemned to die alone. No visitors, no one to comfort the sick. Grieving relatives forced to abandon their loved ones to quarantined rooms.

Result: PANIC

THE FOUR FEARS
COVID

- **FEAR OF UNKNOWN**
- **FEAR OF LOSS**
- **FEAR OF PAIN**
- **FEAR OF FAILURE**

WHY?

GOAL SAVE LIVES — **PANIC** — **STAMP OUT VIRUS**

HOW?

- **EXECUTIVE ORDER**
- **LOCKDOWNS**
- **MANDATES**
- **THREATS**

Fear of Pain

The message was repeated over and over, hour by hour, day by day in the media on television, on the radio - story after story about people dying in the hospital and senior care homes. Examples were cited about people who were on ventilators, or hospitals that did not have ventilators. The airwaves were filled with talking heads citing data of how many infected people there were, or how many more people were going to get infected.

Result: PANIC

Fear of Failure

The command was given that everyone needed to do what the bureaucrats outlined. No one was supposed to leave their house. No one was to congregate. The only way to beat the virus was to lock down. But it was only for a few weeks to stop the spread. This was a temporary "Emergency." The two weeks turned into two months, then unilaterally extended to two years and more.

Result: PANIC

COMMON LAW MAXIM

Words should be considered only as commonly understood and not with a meaning others construe to their own purpose.

Does any reasonable person understand or define the word EMERGENCY as an event or situation that lasts longer than two (2) years?

STAY AT HOME MANDATES

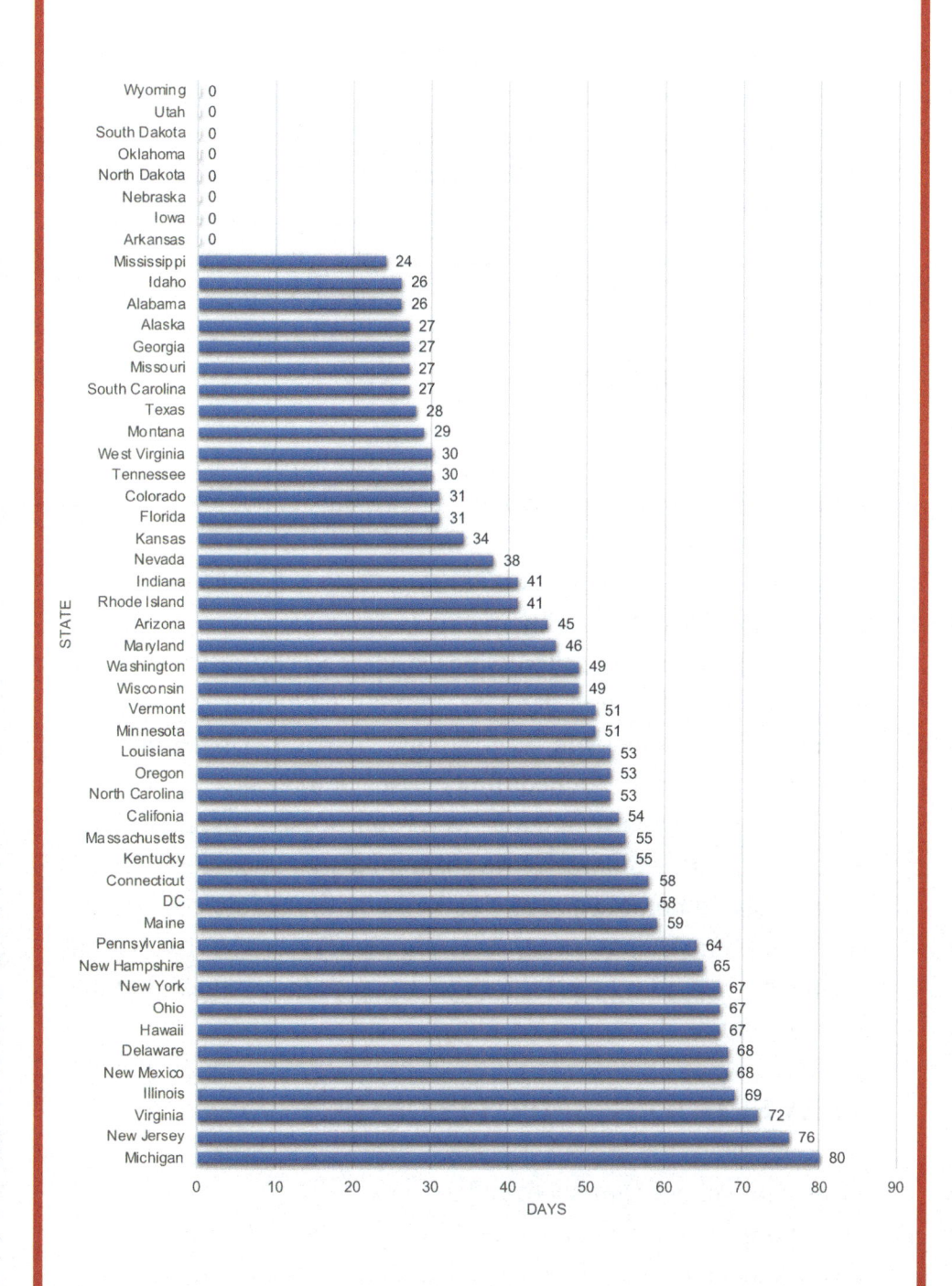

State	Days
Wyoming	0
Utah	0
South Dakota	0
Oklahoma	0
North Dakota	0
Nebraska	0
Iowa	0
Arkansas	0
Mississippi	24
Idaho	26
Alabama	26
Alaska	27
Georgia	27
Missouri	27
South Carolina	27
Texas	28
Montana	29
West Virginia	30
Tennessee	30
Colorado	31
Florida	31
Kansas	34
Nevada	38
Indiana	41
Rhode Island	41
Arizona	45
Maryland	46
Washington	49
Wisconsin	49
Vermont	51
Minnesota	51
Louisiana	53
Oregon	53
North Carolina	53
California	54
Massachusetts	55
Kentucky	55
Connecticut	58
DC	58
Maine	59
Pennsylvania	64
New Hampshire	65
New York	67
Ohio	67
Hawaii	67
Delaware	68
New Mexico	68
Illinois	69
Virginia	72
New Jersey	76
Michigan	80

EVERY SITUATION IS UNIQUE

Only you can answer the questions: what effect did the lockdowns have on you and your family?

Review the chart **STAY AT HOME MANDATES**

Eight states did not issue lockdowns (Stay At Home Mandates). Nine states had lockdowns for 20+ days; Six states for 30 + days; Six states for 40 + days; Eleven states for 50 + days; Eight states for 60 + days; Two states over 70 + days and one state for 80 days.

SCHOOL SHUTDOWNS

Did you know there were many schools that never shut down during the two years the pandemic caused school closures all around the country?

Did you know many schools gave parents a hybrid choice: in classroom attendance or online instruction?

Did you know many schools closed temporarily just until they could make modifications to their campus including rearranging classrooms, erecting safe see-through barriers, installing air purifiers, revising and rescheduling classes outdoors?

Did you know many schools were able to stay open because teachers and staff volunteered to switch classes and schedules so that the most vulnerable and at risk could do the online courses?

Did you know that many schools were manned by parent volunteers when hit by staff shortages because they believed in the importance of in classroom learning?

EVERY SCHOOL CAMPUS IS UNIQUE

Was your school campus open?
Was your child given an option to attend a hybrid class?
Were you given resources so you could help your child online?

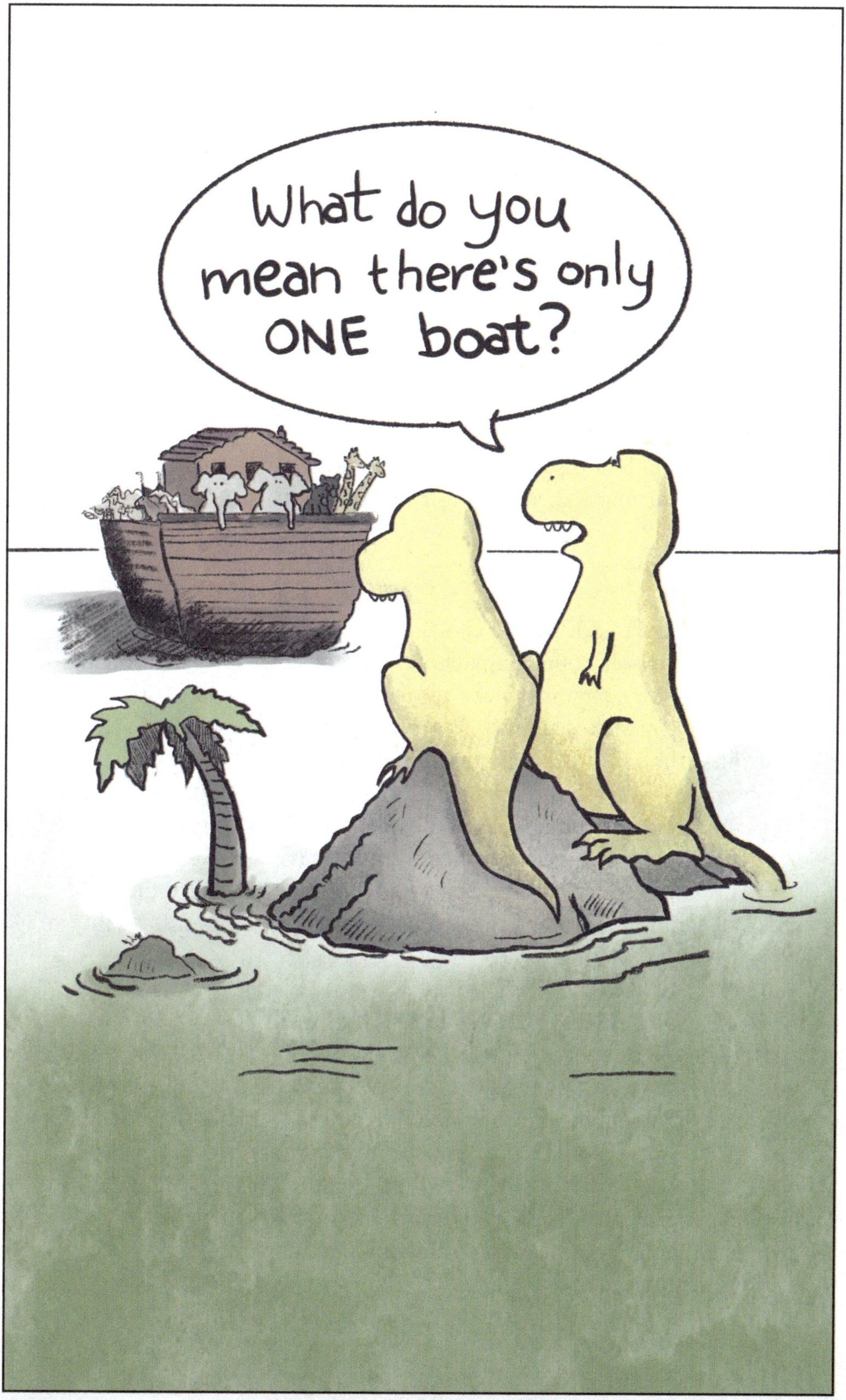
What do you mean there's only ONE boat?

A SECOND OPINION IS A RIGHT

A part of making good decisions requires getting a second opinion no matter the circumstance. With regard to medical cases, it is especially critical that one receive a second opinion. When it comes to your well-being, getting a second opinion will help you decide on an adequate course of treatment. Additionally, receiving multiple opinions dramatically reduces your risk of living with a misdiagnosis and undergoing costly and unnecessary procedures.

Here are the commonsense reasons for getting a second opinion:

• A DEFINITIVE DIAGNOSIS

There are countless diseases that exist today, and many of them share symptoms that make them difficult to differentiate. Symptoms can be caused by more than one disease, so it's best to seek out a specialist that specializes in the symptoms that you are experiencing.

• WE ALL MAKE MISTAKES

For good reason, countless patients hold physicians to a high standard. However, in some circumstances, it can be quite dangerous to do so. Even doctors make mistakes at times. When they are juggling multiple patients in so little time, a mishap is unfortunate but inevitable. If you are not satisfied with your doctor's diagnosis or you feel that you have not been properly cared for, you should immediately begin seeking out a second opinion. Furthermore, it is not necessary to have a reason to request a second opinion. Take confidence in knowing that you have the right to seek out multiple opinions until you are satisfied with your quality of care.

• EXPLORE TREATMENT OPTIONS

But maybe proper diagnosis is not your issue. Perhaps you are satisfied with your diagnosis but are unclear on the treatment options that are available to you. Many conditions have a plethora of available treatments. For example: physical therapy, surgery, medication are all types of treatment that can be used for the same disease – but it depends on the patient. That is why it is important for you to have a clear understanding of your health and body in order to make the best decision on your treatment.

THOROUGH UNDERSTANDING

Perhaps the most vital component of seeking out a second opinion is the importance of understanding your medical history. Some doctors don't take enough time for a thorough examination which often leads to a misdiagnosis. Studies show that most doctors spend twenty minutes or less with each patient. In may cases, this is not enough time to get all of your concerns properly addressed.

QUESTIONS THAT MUST BE ASKED

1. Why were second opinions on treatment for Covid 19 ignored or discredited without cause?

2. Why were people not encouraged to seek counsel from their family physicians on treatment?

3. Why were approaches recommended by family physicians who know their patients best disregarded?

4. Why were there no educational programs emphasizing how to improve people's immune systems to protect against Covid 10

Challenging a diagnosis and treatment is a great way to further understand the accuracy of what has been said, rather than accepting the message because of who said it.

In fact, many studies prove this very point: a second opinion results in changing the diagnosis 15% of the time, and changes the treatment 37% of the time.

By obtaining a second opinion, whether on a local or national scale – a patient would ensure being diagnosed appropriately. This would increase the chances that the patient would receive the most up-to-date and optimal treatment plan.

Did You Know?

From John's Hopkins Hospital regarding the Covid19 virus…

- **This virus is not a living organism.** It is a protein molecule (RNA or DNA covered by a protective layer of lipid (fat), which, when absorbed by the cells of the ocular (eyes), nasal (nose) or buccal mucosa (mouth), changes their genetic code (mutates) and converts into aggressor and multiplier cells.
- Since the virus is not a living organism, but is a protein molecule, it cannot be killed. It has to decay on its own. **The disintegration time depends on the temperature, humidity and type of material where it lies**.
- **The virus is very fragile; the only thing that protects it is a thin outer layer of fat, and that is the reason why soap or detergent is the best weapon. The foam CUTS THE FAT (that is why you have to scrub for 20 seconds or more, to create lots of foam). By dissolving the fat layer, the protein molecule disperses and breaks down**.
- **HEAT** melts fat; this is why it is necessary to use water above 77 degrees for hand washing, laundry and cleaning surfaces. In addition, hot water makes more foam, making it more effective.
- **Alcohol** or any mixture with alcohol over 65% DISSOLVES ALL FAT, especially the external lipid layer of the virus.
- **Any solution with 1 part bleach and 5 parts water directly dissolves the protein, breaking it down from the inside**.
- NO BACTERICIDE OR ANTIBIOTIC WILL WORK because the virus is not a complete living organism like bacteria; antibiotics cannot kill what is not alive.
- The virus molecules remain very stable at colder temperatures, including air conditioning in houses and cars. They also need moisture and darkness to stay stable. Therefore, dehumidified, dry, warm and bright environments will degrade the virus faster.
- UV LIGHT on any object that may contain the virus breaks down the protein. Be careful, it also breaks down collagen (which is protein) in the skin.
- The virus CANNOT go through healthy skin.
- Vinegar is NOT useful because it does not break down the protective layer of fat.
- NO SPIRITS, NOR VODKA, serve. The strongest vodka is only 40% alcohol, and you need a minimum of 65%.
- LISTERINE is 65% alcohol.
- The more confined the space, the concentration of the virus will be higher. The more open or naturally ventilated, the less.

COMMON SENSE OBSERVATIONS

In February of 2020, based on the findings distributed by John Hopkins Hospital regarding COVID 19, these observations gave us the key on how to deal with this new coronavirus.

WHAT IS COVID 19?

The virus is not a living bacteria, it is a protein molecule protected by a thin layer of fat. By dissolving the fat layer, the protein layer breaks down. It cannot penetrate healthy skin, so it attacks the body through the T-Zone : the eyes, the nose and the mouth. Once in the body, the virus mutates and multiplies.

WHERE DOES THE VIRUS THRIVE?

The virus molecules love moisture and darkness. Colder temperatures, especially in airconditioned homes and cars keep the molecules stable and happy. The more confined the space, the concentration of the virus will be higher.

HOW TO PREVENT THE VIRUS FROM MULTIPLYING

Dehumidified, dry, warm and bright environments are best. Open, naturally ventilated outdoor spaces are even better.

HOW TO ATTACK THE VIRUS

Bactericide and antibiotics will not work on a virus. Best weapon is soap and water above 77 degrees. UV light breaks down the protein. Alcohol with a minimum of 65%. Listerine is 65%.

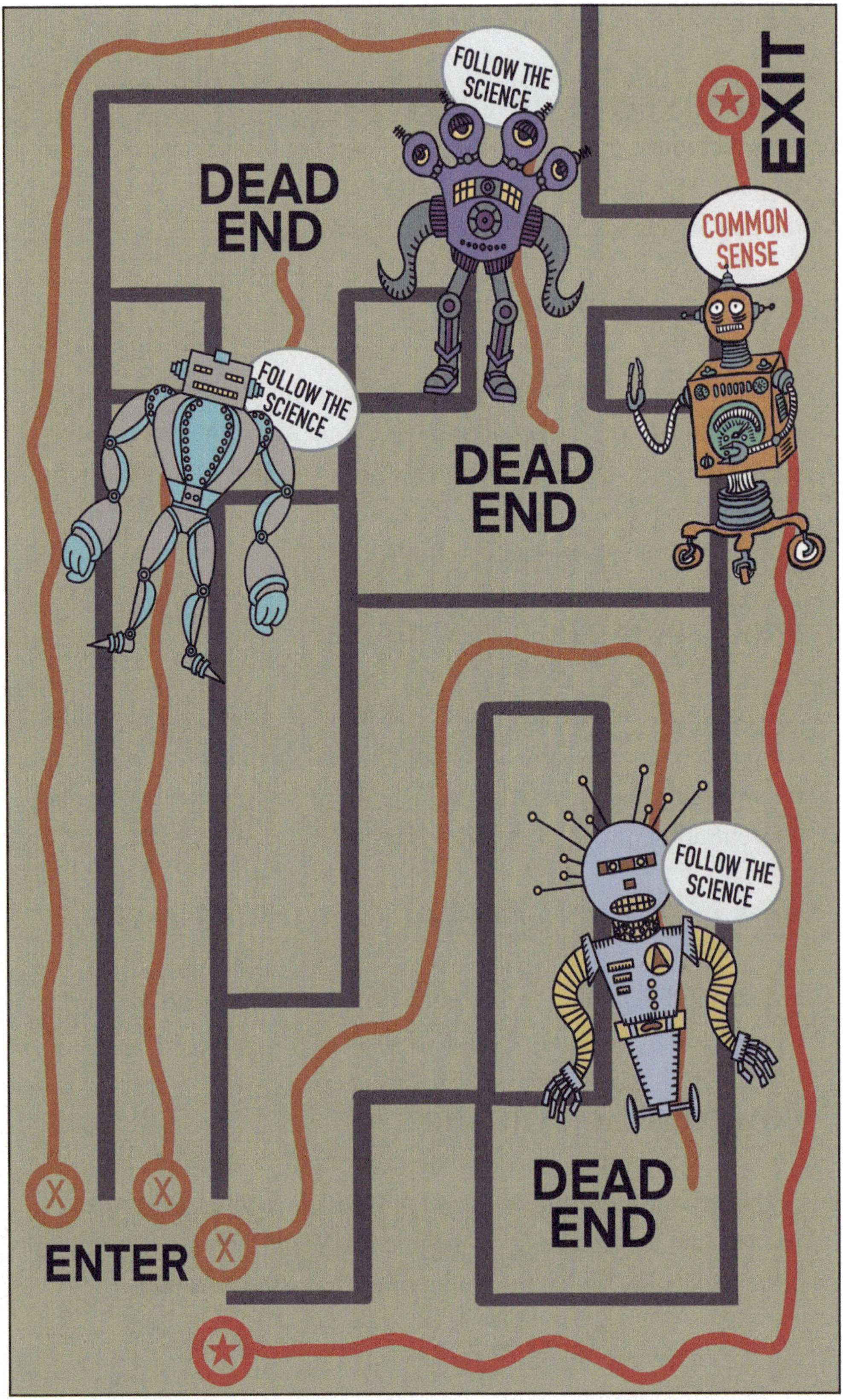
FOLLOW THE SCIENCE
DEAD END
EXIT
COMMON SENSE
FOLLOW THE SCIENCE
DEAD END
FOLLOW THE SCIENCE
DEAD END
ENTER

Who is the Biggest Bully?

FOLLOW THE SCIENCE

What does "Follow the Science" mean ? It is a non-sequitur, pardon the pun.

Science is simply an organized system of testing theories to acquire and arrive at a body of knowledge.

Bureaucrats pretend that there is no other option than to follow the knowledge presented to them by the scientists. In reality, leaders make decisions and choices based not only on the present knowledge but also on a multitude of other factors beyond just data. In other words, people need to make the decisions.

EXAMPLES OF BUREAUCRATIC DECISIONS

Our examples are based only on actual experiences or events we personally witnessed.

- SENIORS MUST STAY INDOORS

- NEIGHBORHOOD PARKS

Yellow tape blocking all entrances to the parks. Newly erected signs posted at the entrances with the WARNING that there will be a $ 10,000 fine for anyone entering the park.

- PUBLIC BEACHES

No person is allowed to sit, lie or play on the sand or any portion of any public beach.

Remember that these proclamations were based on the "science" which we just observed in DID YOU KNOW? Despite the advisory that the worst place to be is gathered indoors in air conditioning, the best place to be is outdoors in the bright, warm, sun enjoying the breezes.

Destructive Consequences

- MENTAL ILLNESS
- BULLYCIDE
- DRUG OVERDOSE

OUR STUDENTS

- BROKEN RELATIONSHIPS
- LOSS OF EDUCATION OPPORTUNITIES
- BROKEN DREAMS

UNINTENDED CONSEQUENCES

Our reaction to the global COVID-19 pandemic is responsible for a host of negative developments that are disrupting lives all over the world – from lost jobs and emotional scars and death. Let's take a closer look at the negative consequences that were unintentionally placed upon our school-aged children.

ELEMENTARY SCHOOL CHILDREN

In a time of crisis, younger kids are often the most vulnerable. With the current state of the nation, many students are behind in the basic curricula. The pandemic lockdown forced many children to miss out on valuable childhood experiences. Due to stay-at-home orders, students were forced to learn academic material on their own with the help of parents instead of being face-to-face with a teacher. Though online learning became prominent, many of these young students and their parents may not have been technologically savvy enough to learn the material required. This resulted in loss of learning as well as development issues. In fact, anxiety, grief and depression often resulted in disruptive behavior. The lack of emotional maturity led to frustrations in the form of bullying and violence.

MIDDLES SCHOOL CHILDREN

Middle school students suffered significantly. One of the most notable consequences of staying at home led to emotional distress, trauma, and mental health issues like depression.

Middle school-ages children are especially vulnerable to these risks because they are not yet fully mature enough to handle these feelings by themselves. These students were used to going to school every day and socializing with their friends. Then, all of a sudden, the bond between teachers and friends was ripped from their daily routine leaving them confused, isolated and suffering the panic of loneliness. This trauma altered the personality and mental health of countless students who have to learn to be themselves again.

HIGH SCHOOL STUDENTS

High school students had the most difficult time coping with the stay- at-home orders. The stringent lockdowns resulted in students missing their once-in-a-lifetime events such as proms and graduation as well as losing valuable opportunities for academic grants and athletic scholarships. The increase in mental health problems, overdoses, suicides, and emotional problems is a direct result of keeping schools closed.

High school students lost the joy of participating in extra curricular with friends, they also lost the ability to work part time jobs. This increased the burden of financial pressure on families who were unable to prepare for college tuition as they had originally planned. Now as these students prepare to move forward in their lives, they are showing increased signs of stress from the trauma experienced during the pandemic.

The long-term effects of school lockdowns will be felt over the course of many years. The two year delay for evidence based reality is coming home to roost.

INTELLIGENT DISOBEDIENCE

- **BLINK**
- **THINK**
- **CHOICE**
- **VOICE**

A VALUABLE TECHNIQUE
TO STAND UP TO BULLIES

RECOMMENDED FOR ALL AGES

INTELLIGENT DISOBEDIENCE

Ira Chaleff developed a new technique for keeping children safe. The skill set is taught to children and is invaluable in the training of guide dogs and service dogs. For example, we teach our children not to get into a stranger's car or walk off with someone in the shopping mall. But what if it is a person of authority that is telling them to do something they shouldn't? Today, we believe that people of all ages should learn this skill on recognizing when we need to say NO rather than go along with something we believe is wrong even though the bureaucrats demand that we do so.

BLINK

Did you hear the person of authority right? Pause. Register what you heard. Consider your disbelief in what is being asked of you to do. Do not be bullied by social pressure of your peers or friends figure.

THINK

Why are you being asked to do this? Is it contrary to what you have been taught by your parents, your teachers, your family, your church? Is it beneficial to you? Is it harmful to you or anyone else if you comply?

CHOICE

YOU have a choice. You can choose to obey, you can choose to disobey, you can offer another option, you can ask for time to decide, you can ask to check with someone else first. Which choice seems right at the moment?

VOICE

If your conscience helps you decide to say NO, say it loud and clear. NO means NO.

THE MOTHER TERESA OF D.C. STANDS UP TO BULLY BUREAUCRATS

A Hero's History

Sister Deirdre Byrne lovingly referred to as Sister Dede, but perhaps best recognized as "Mother Teresa" of Washington, D.C. has no problem standing her ground. Sister Dede is a renowned physician-surgeon as well as a retired United States Army colonel.

She is also a Roman Catholic nun who is an active missionary sister in addition to a superior of her community in Washington, DC.

Sister Dede grew up in the suburbs of Washington in McLean, Virginia. She was raised by a large, devout Catholic family. As a graduate of Virginia Tech, she attended Georgetown School of Medicine and joined the United States Army as a medical student soon after.

That began a career of selfless acts including serving as a full-time officer for 13 months in the Sinai Peninsula as well as volunteering to serve in Korea in order to practice family and emergency medicine.

She has risked her life in war zones for the betterment of the residents. For example, she has performed surgery on the ground after disasters in Kenya, Afghanistan, Haiti, Iraq and Sudan.

In Washington D.C., she continued to serve as the medical director of her convent's free medical clinic.

A Hero's Hardship

But despite her history of sacrifices and excellent leadership in her community, she was denied a religious exemption to the District of Columbia's COVID-19 vaccination mandate for health care workers. The policy includes exemptions for medical or religious reasons, Sister Dede's application was denied. Sister Dede learned via a letter that her request was denied and that her medical license was suspended.

As a result, her attorneys filed a suit in the federal United States District Court on her behalf, against Washington D.C., Mayor Muriel Bowser, and the director of the district's health department.

It's important to note that none of the medical practices where Sister Dede volunteered, ever expressed any objection to her religious beliefs against the vaccine.

The alleged reason for the denial is "undue hardship". Sister Dede's legal team offers the rebuttal that she had previously contracted Covid-19 and remains naturally immune to the virus. Furthermore, DC|Health does not employ sister Dede and they cannot suffer any hardship by offering an exemption.

Battle Against Bully Bureaucrats

After Sister Dede sued Washington, D.C., and the mayor, reprieve was eventually granted. Although that is a temporary fix to one problem, it doesn't resolve all of the issues raised in her lawsuit.

Though she can now resume seeing patients, it is not the end of the story. The debate has been sparked as to whether Sister Dede is being treated differently than others who object to such mandates. It is also being questioned what exactly the letter meant which indicated that she is able to practice unless it is not in the "best interest of public health". It is also unclear as to who makes such as decision.

Yet, still in her hardships, Sister Dede is using her prominence and her faith as a driving force to serve others. While Sister Dede's legal team has been in the process of discussing these issues with other attorneys, she announced her plan to reopen her medical clinic and has scheduled surgeries. Although she is able to practice medicine again, she is determined to raise awareness for other medical professionals who have religious objections to the vaccine.

In the beautiful words of Sister Dede, "I really don't want this to be my own little battle."

Bureaucrat	vs	Leader
Mandates		Options
Only One Way		Situation Determines Solution
No Responsibility		Accountable
Confusing		Clear
No Explanation		Common Sense
Unresponsive		Responsive
Because We Said So		Reasonable Explanation
Untimely		Prompt
Conflicting Data		Updated Data
Manipulative		Cooperative
Blame Game		Flexible

EMERGENCY POWER

Compare our chart Bureaucrat vs. Leader. Every location is unique. Only you can review your own personal experience over the last two and a half years during the pandemic. Did you have a Bureaucrat or a Leader running your school, your school board, your church, your town, your city, your state?

Look at the check list of eleven characteristics on the comparative chart, would you check more under the Bureaucrat or more under the Leader for each category?

Here is a surefire way to determine if you were being manipulated or given options to find the best solution for your situation. How long was the "Emergency Status "used in your school, city or state?

Words should be considered only as commonly understood and not with a meaning others construe to their own purpose.

If everyone else around you, your neighboring town, city or state, dropped the "Emergency Status" regarding the Covid restrictions, then you should probably realize the word "Emergency" was only being used as a legal ruse to extend the control and access to funding and other benefits.

Anytime we use words to deceive others under the pretense of an "emergency" we are using deceitful tactics. The purpose is to gain an advantage over others who trust the people in authority to do the right thing at the right time.

DO YOU GET IT NOW?

The Golden Circle

Why

How

What

"And it's those who start with "WHY" that have the ability to inspire those around them…we follow those who lead, not because we have to, but because we want to."

– Golden Circle by Simon Sinek

CRYSTAL BALL?

Confronted by critics especially angry parents, bureaucrats argue it's not their fault. They protest that they had no way of knowing what they did would cause the destructive consequences that happened during the pandemic. They claim that no one can see the future. Punxsutawney's success rate is better than theirs.

Can we see into the future? If your answer is "No" then why do we tell people a week in advance, sometimes two weeks that they need to leave the comfort of their homes because a hurricane with force winds of 140 miles per hour is heading directly at them. Looking up at the clear skies and beautiful sunshine, most people heed the weather man's warning because they understand the prediction may not be 100% accurate in timing or path, but the risk is too great to ignore.

Could we not then predict the disastrous consequences of the mandates in place in many of our cities and towns?

- Confine senior citizens to stay indoors
- Lockdown schools and churches
- Close neighborhood parks and community centers
- Restrict access to public beaches
- Shut down mom & pops but keep the megastores open

Could we not foresee the increase in drug overdoses, mental illness, broken relationships, broken dreams and our children 's loss of learning?

Yes, common sense, shared wisdom, technology and inspiration tells us so.

PUNXSUTAWNEY PHIL

> **OUT DAMNED SPOT! OUT I SAY!**
>
> – Lady Macbeth (Act v, Scene 1)

PART 5

FIX IT!

> Do the best you can till you know better. Then, when you know better, Do better.
>
> – Maya Angelou

Creative minds find solutions.

Practical minds produce results.

United minds achieve success.

– A. J. Lactaoen

A DIFFERENT WAY

" Not until we are lost, do we begin to find ourselves."

What we did the past two years during the pandemic, was destructive to the most vulnerable of us – our seniors and our children. We need to find a different way to confront our challenges.

CREATIVE MINDS FIND SOLUTIONS

We need to tap into the genius of our society. First of all, we need to recognize that the old way of doing things is not the only way or even the best way. We need the wisdom of our past experience but also the creativity of our brightest. We need to relinquish the hold that our bureaucratic "experts" have on us and reach out to the talented who approach problems from a different perspective. We need to place more emphasis on what is being said rather than be influenced by who says it. We need to take a comprehensive approach to a pandemic as more than a health crisis – we need to invite representatives from all the disciplines including medicine, science, psychology, education, local government, business and faith based organizations.

PRACTICAL MINDS PRODUCE RESULTS

To achieve results, these are required:

- Accountability
- Transparency
- Neutrality
- Timeliness

Problem Solving Approach

Common Sense	Shared Wisdom
Technology	Inspiration

Situation Determines The Solution

PROBLEM SOLVING APPROACH

COMMON SENSE

Beware of illogical, non-sensical rule making bureaucrats who insist on countering good old fashion wisdom. Instead of posting and enforcing rules like preventing people from walking their dog, remind them of the precepts they should have learned from Gramma:

- Stay Home when you are sick
- Less is better (Stay away from groups)
- It Takes 2 (It's all right to jog alone)
- It Does Not Have to Be Either / Or (Know your options)

SHARED WISDOM

Tap into the insights of everyone who has information, suggestions, knowledge. Do not ignore the obvious. Why would we not listen to a long time family doctor who has treated hundreds of children but take the word of a non-practicing researcher on how to treat a patient?

TECHNOLOGY

Use the data we are able to tap into because of technology but do not fall into the trap of "following the science" which so many have done. Data is information. People make the decisions that affect all of us. In order to avoid accountability, bureaucrats blame the "science."

INSPIRATION

Leaders know how to use all of the tools at their disposal to make wise decisions.

That includes a common sense born from experience, taking into account suggestions and counsel from trusted advisors, current data and information gathered by the best technology and the one unidentifiable thing that bureaucrats never understand – an inspiration to try a novel approach from a different perspective or an "AHA" moment in time.

OVERCOMING THE FOUR FEARS OF COVID

What if we had approached the Four Fears of the Pandemic in a different way. You are the only one that can make the decision if it is a better way given your own unique circumstance.

WHAT IF WE CHOSE ANOTHER WAY ?

The Bureaucratic Way was highlighted by:

- Executive Orders
- Lockdowns
- Mandates
- Threats

The Common Sense Approach Way:
- Developing A Comprehensive Strategy with All Options Available

- Using a multi-prong instead of a one-way approach
- Recognizing the uniqueness of each location
- Modeling what works

THE FOUR FEARS
COVID

- FEAR OF UNKNOWN
- FEAR OF LOSS
- FEAR OF PAIN
- FEAR OF FAILURE

WHY?
GOAL
SAVE LIVES

COMPREHENSIVE STRATEGIES

HOW?
FOCUS ON VULNERABLE

- ALL TOOLS ALL OPTIONS
- SHARED WISDOM
- SITUATION DETERMINES SOLUTION
- MODEL WHAT WORKS

A BETTER WAY

What if instead of locking down our schools, we kept them open and initiated the Comprehensive Strategy that proved to be very successful for those campuses that stayed open. Did your neighborhood school shut down or stay open?

PROACTIVE EDUCATIONAL WORKSHOPS

- Invite parents and guests to participate in workshops to learn how best to prevent Covid 19 from spreading

- Review the protocols the school was taking as preventative measures and offer suggestions on how families could do the same

- Emphasize the importance of checking with their family doctor and following their physician's advice on treatment including antiviral, antibody and vaccine options

- Discuss the types of masks that are most effective (N95, K95, Cloth)

CREATE NEW SCHEDULES WITH OPTIONS

- Set up rotating on campus instruction

- Offer courses to students and parents on how to do online classes

- Design a hybrid instructional system with some students on campus and some online.

MODIFY THE STRUCTURE AND USE OF CLASSROOMS

- Whenever possible, schedule classes outdoors

- Arrange desks in strategic design to take advantage of transparent barriers

- Use of technological tools such as temperature walk ins, UV-C lights, etc.

Comprehensive Strategy

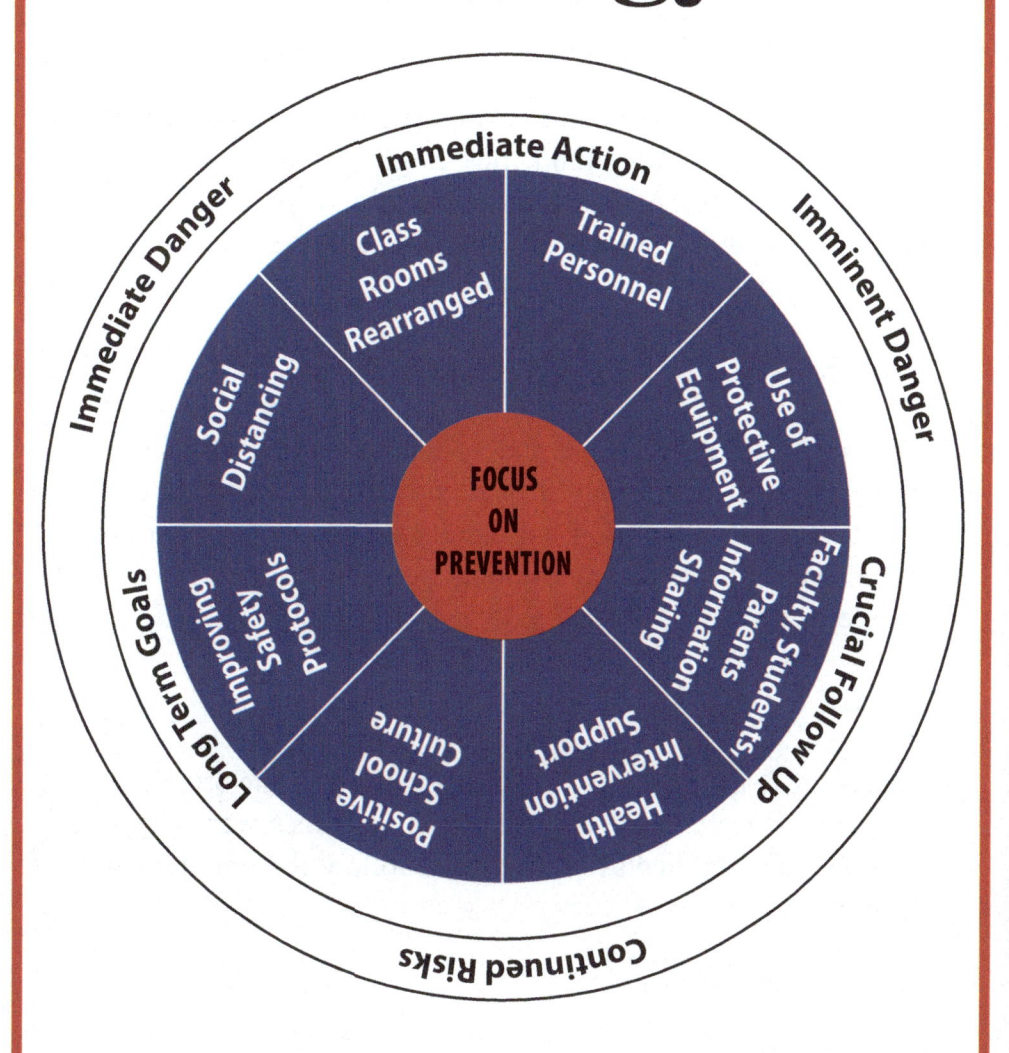

- **Immediate Action**
  - Class Rooms Rearranged
  - Trained Personnel
- **Imminent Danger**
  - Use of Protective Equipment
  - Faculty, Students, Parents Information Sharing
- **Crucial Follow Up**
  - Health Intervention Support
  - Positive School Culture
- **Continued Risks**
  - Improving Safety Protocols
  - Social Distancing
- **Immediate Danger**
- **Long Term Goals**

FOCUS ON PREVENTION

TO PREVENT COVID-19 SPREAD

THE DISCIPLINE OF SETTING PRIORITIES

In our emergency first aid classes, we describe a scenario where they find three victims of an accident: one victim is moaning and bleeding profusely; one victim is crying and screaming in terror; one victim looks to be unconscious and not breathing. Our question is which victim do you need to attend to first ?

Unfortunately, many want to choose the victim that is bleeding profusely although they admit they might go to the one who is screaming the loudest first. Obviously after explaining the time emergency involved they realize that CPR and the use of the AED on the unconscious victim is top priority.

TRIAGE

The principle of Triage is the system of setting priorities and organizing and classifying the victims in the order and time frame they need attention. First responders practice this principle established during war zones long ago in deadly events with multiple victims.

TRIAGE for COVID 19

For some reason, during the pandemic it seems the principle was turned on its head. More emphasis and resources were expended doing tests for the healthy rather than follow the common sense priority:

- TREAT THE SICK

- EDUCATE THE VULNERABLE

- EMPOWER THE HEALTHY (To help the sick and teach the vulnerable)

TRIAGE *For* COVID-19
THE COMMON SENSE WAY

DEGREES OF PRIORITIES

Category 1: IMMEDIATE
Treat The Sick

Category 2: URGENT
Educate the Vulnerable

Category 3: NON-URGENT
Empower the Healthy

SILVER LINING

Do you believe that behind every dark cloud there is a silver lining? Some people think that the pandemic actually struck gold for unbelieving parents who were able to witness for themselves what their children were being forced to endure.

LOCKOUTS AND MANDATES

Here is where the curtains were pulled back and the reality hit parents between the eyes. Some schools shut down their campuses and relied strictly on ZOOM for children to engage with their teachers to learn their lessons. Because many parents were also at home due to the shutdown of workplaces, they observed first hand what their children were being taught.

Many parents were delighted to help and participate in the virtual lessons, thankful for the teacher who spent double time preparing lessons online.

But too many parents from K-12 discovered for the first time, the agenda that was being forced on the students contrary to their family beliefs, values and practices.

Parents and Teachers are the best thing between children and harm's way

---

MAMA & PAPA BEARS ARE WOKEN

Mellow, patient, kind people intentionally avoid confrontation. They go the extra mile to be cooperative, even compliant. But if they see you harming their children, they turn from reluctant to compelled defenders of their young.

They will be the primary leaders challenging the Culture Wars and supporting the importance of Content and Character in the war on education.

Don't poke a mama bear!

TAKE BACK THE POWER

Before "Harry Potter" and "Star War" when our kids were growing up, the most popular trilogy of the time was "Back to the Future" staring Michael J. Fox. The intriguing point of the series was that one defining moment – Macfly (Fox's Dad) either saves his Mom by standing up to the big bully at the high school dance or wimps out and passes up the chance. The choice he makes will affect the future of their family, their friends and their community for generations.

Luckily for us, we have the capability of making choices in midstream. We can change our minds and get back on track if we find we have made a mistake. Sometimes it's difficult, sometimes not. We do however, in our personal lives have that choice.

The big problem in our society today is that when it concerns our interrelations with one another, we have either given up our power altogether or we don't realize the strength each one of us has collectively. There is that defining moment when we will lose our chance to change our minds forever.

What if we had the magic to ride that special wing-door car back to the future and we found our grandchildren now grown up living in bombed out shelters with sickness and disease every where? What if we found our cities and towns scarred by the horrors of war, no flower, no grass, the trees dead because the sunlight can't get through the clouds heavy with pollution? What if our rivers and streams and lakes were poisoned or dried up? What if there were no more schools open for our children, no hospitals for our sick, no homes for our elderly, no police force or firemen to help the needy?

What if I told you the defining moment that changed the future was the day you and I didn't take the time to vote? That particular year changed the make-up of the city council or the House of Representatives, of the Senate and the Presidency. That particular year new judges were appointed for life. That particular year new bills were introduced and passed as law. That particular year the Supreme Court ruled on life changing decisions which set in motion a series of events which would alter the fabric of society as we know it.

Again, this is something we are never taught in school. Yet the impact on our lives can and will be felt for generations. Your vote is not for the person who wins the election. It is for how that one person whose values and beliefs can affect the course of history will stand up for our principles or not. Your vote gives that person the platform and the key to enter into a hallowed chamber. It can be a chamber of horrors or the halls of justice and fairness.

In the final analysis, you and I will be the ultimate decision makers. For the sake of our children and grandchildren. VOTE.

Vote for your neighborhood School Board. Vote for your school Parent Teacher Organization. Vote for your City Council. Vote for your Mayor, Vote for your State House & Senate. Vote for your State representatives to Congress. When the time comes, Vote for the Vice-President and President. Vote and tell your children whom you voted for and why. VOTE.

> "We have met the enemy, and he is us."
>
> – Walt Kelly, aka Pogo

RIGHT MAKES MIGHT

Some schools believe if they put up signs all around the campus that say

BULLY FREE ZONE, then the students will believe them. Some businesses believe that if they include in their company handbook the warning BULLIES NOT ALLOWED, then the personnel will believe them.

BYSTANDER SUPPORT

Kids know that policies, slogans, and posters don't count. What helps is an administration who actively engages in promoting and supporting the main ingredient to stop bullying – the Bystander who supports the victim and stands up against the bully. The Bystander can be an ally of the Bully or an ally of the Victim. They need the encouragement to choose wisely.

As an example, in order to demonstrate to the whole student body the dynamic of right makes might, we call up the smallest student in the high school division to come up on stage. Next we call the biggest, toughest looking student to face the first student in a Tug-O-War contest with a thick rope on stage. The contest is easily won by the bigger stronger student who can pull the flag over the finish line with one hand.

We then call up 6-10 mores students to come up and help the smaller student who lost. This time, the bigger victor needs two arms and a longer time to pull the flag over to his side. He still wins. The third contest now features another group of 6-10 students added to the losing side. This time, there is no question. The team of bystanders turned participants help the smaller, weaker student to victory.

The lesson is clear to the whole student body. No Bully can withstand the force of people working together.

Parents must use the principle of right makes right by uniting those who are being bullied unfairly by bureaucrats

Stand Up To The Bully

Bully against 1

Bully against 10

Bully against 25

S T O P

This is what we advise all of our participants to do in our emergency workshops.

SITUATION

Assess the situation. What kind of emergency are we facing?

Our children are being bullied.

THINK

How are the children being harmed? Who is doing the harm?

The Bullies are the Bureaucrats in authority.

OPTIONS

To Protect our children:

a. Remove them from the school
b. Challenge the Bureaucrats

PLAN

Fight back. Become a Mama and Papa Bear and take **ACTION**.

GO TO THE SOURCE

Our experience working with teachers on every level K-12 is that they welcome the participation of parents, grandparent, custodians, support relatives. Why wouldn't they? Experienced teachers know that family support encourages their students to be the best they can be and makes their job easier and more rewarding. New teachers learn very quickly that they need all the help they can get in dealing with their students.

RED FLAG

If you hear unpleasant news from fellow parents, friends, colleagues about what is happening in your child's school, get your antennae up but DO NOT ASSUME.

VERIFY AND CORROBORATE

Go direct to the source. Talk to your child's teacher. Talk to your child's Principal.

Participate in the Parents Teacher Association. Read the school's newsletter and check the school's website and social media.

Use the Buddy System we teach our kids. If you feel you need support, join up with a fellow parent or a parent's group – you don't need to do this alone.

FOLLOW PROTOCOL

If written communication is required, write it and make sure you save copies.

DOCUMENT

Preserve all written correspondence, record all dates and times of meetings and phone conversations. Note down names and bystanders of any event.

GO TO THE SOURCE!

ACTION PLAN

" There are always three sides to a story. Yours, Theirs and the Truth."

If you have done everything you can to mediate the dispute, and you are left with no other viable options to stand up to the Bullies to protect your children.

SUE 'UM

Use the most powerful power the people have as a tool to force the Bureaucrats to keep their promise to the people. The courts belong to you not the Bureaucrats. The courts belong to your family, your friends, your neighbors. The courts belong to everyone. Our courts exist to serve the people. Our courts provide the venue where the people come to state their grievances so they can receive the remedies that justice requires. There is no room for Bullies in the people's courts.

LIST OF QUOTES

1. POLITICAL SCIENCE 29
2. 12 ANGRY MEN 38
3. MARTIN LUTHER KING 40
4. MERCHANT OF VENICE 59
5. THE PIANIST 67
6. STRONG PEOPLE 70
7. LADY MACBETH 120
8. MINDS – AJL 122

LIST OF FLYERS

1. DO YOU AGREE 13
2. WE ARE VESTED 15
3. COMMON SENSE PRINCIPLES 23
4. CIRCLE OF INFLUENCE 24
5. BETRAYED 26
6. HELICOPTER 31
7. FOCUS 33
8. RULE OF BENJAMIN 35
9. ADVICE TO PARENTS 36
10. MANY FACES OF TRUTH 47
11. WHOM DO YOU BELIEVE 51
12. GLOBAL TRUST 52
13. LEAST TRUSTED 53

14. ELEPHANT	55
15. TIME	57
16. FACT OR FICTION	72
17. BEST TO END BULLY	75
18. PROFILES	77
19. HIERARCHY OF NEEDS	79
20. ANATOMY	81
21. UNANSWERED QUESTIONS	82
22. COVID	90
23. FOUR FEARS PANIC	97
24. STAY AT HOME	99
25. DINOSAUR	101
26. DID YOU KNOW	104
27. ROBOTS	106
28. DESTRUCTIVE CONSEQUENCES	108
29. INTELLIGENT DISOBEDIENCE	111
30. BUREAUCRAT VS. LEADER	115
31. GOLDEN CIRCLE	117
32. PUNXSUTAWNEY PHIL	119
33. PROBLEM SOLVING	124
34. TRIAGE	131
35. MAMA BEAR	133
36. STAND UP	137
37. GO TO THE SOURCE	140

PREVIEW

WHO IS THE BIGGEST BULLY OF ALL?
BOOK 2 : CONTENT & CHARACTER
WHAT ARE WE TEACHING OUR CHILDREN?

We believe in the goodwill and professionalism of our schools. Parents trusted that schools were giving their children the best possible education while keeping them safe. Sadly, today parents need to verify what schools are teaching their children. The pandemic opened a pandora's box which exposed a dark secret. What are these schools hiding?

"There are two ways to be fooled. One is to believe what isn't true; the other is to refuse to believe what is true."
— Kierkegaard

- Is your school teaching CRT – aka Critical Race Theory? Why?
- Is your school teaching gender identity to K-3 students? Why?
- Is your school forcing girls to use the same bathrooms as biological males?
- Is your school allowing trans athletes to compete against girl athletes?
- Is your school eliminating advanced placement courses?
- Is your school using race as the basis of selection rather than merit?
- Is your school encouraging parent participation?
- Is your school bullying students to join in activist causes?
- Is your school focusing on the core academic subjects?

PREVIEW

WHO IS THE BIGGEST BULLY OF ALL?
BOOK 3 : CULTURE WARS
WHY ARE WE CONFUSING OUR CHILDREN?

We are all guilty in contributing to the trauma we are putting our children through during a time in their lives when they should be celebrating the joy of learning and experimentation. This situation is not true for all schools, but it seems the problem is more than just isolated to a few random campuses.

" Children learn as they play. More importantly, in play, children learn how to learn."

— Fred Donaldson

In K-3 grades, are our children allowed to play and revel in getting to know new friends, or are we focusing on race preference and gender identity?

In our middle schools, when our children are coping with cyber-bullying and coming of age crushes, are we letting them experiment with their favorite subjects like science and robotics or are we scaring them to death with the prospect of climate change end of the world doom?

In our high schools, instead of emphasizing the prospects of college or workforce choices, are we depressing these vulnerable new adults with solving the problems of abortion, cancel culture, and social media exploitation?

We maybe are not directly involved in this abuse, but those who have not stood up to challenge this travesty are complicit. Join us in making your voices heard.

Made in the USA
Columbia, SC
26 November 2022